SHARK

Shark-tooth gauntlet,
Kiribati, western
Pacific Ocean

Pair of copepods, which
stick onto sharks' fins

Undulate ray

Angel shark

Model of a male
great white shark

Pair of baby dogfish

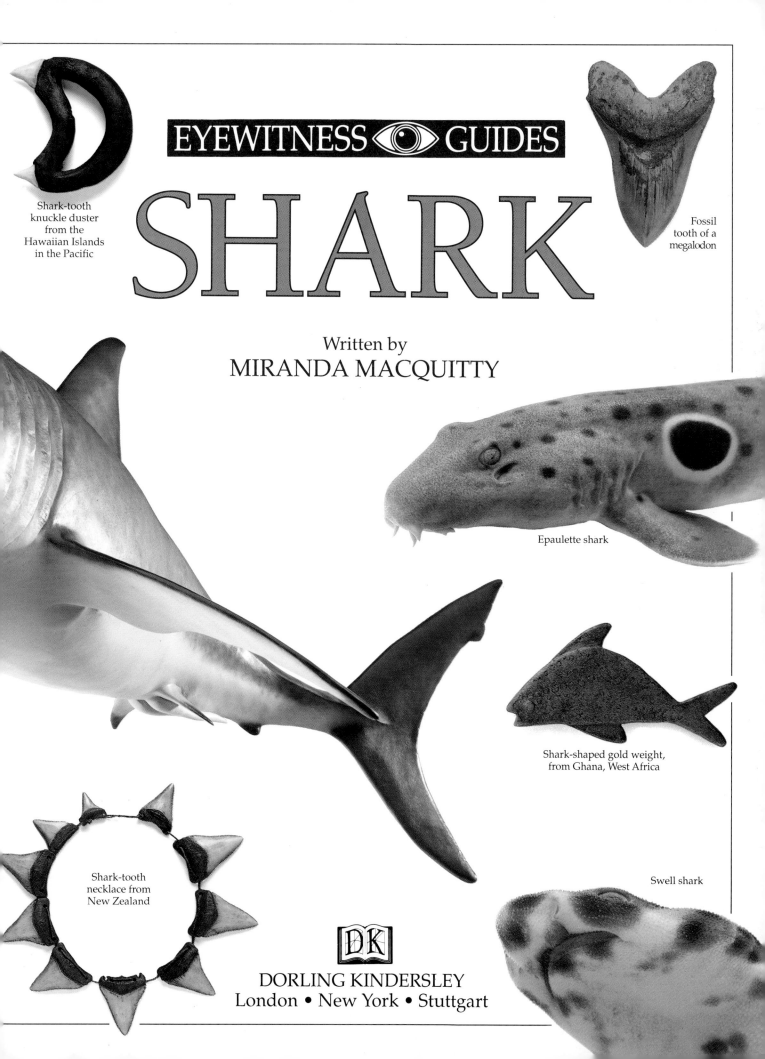

Shark-tooth
knuckle duster
from the
Hawaiian Islands
in the Pacific

EYEWITNESS 👁 GUIDES
SHARK

Fossil
tooth of a
megalodon

Written by
MIRANDA MACQUITTY

Epaulette shark

Shark-shaped gold weight,
from Ghana, West Africa

Shark-tooth
necklace from
New Zealand

Swell shark

DK

DORLING KINDERSLEY
London • New York • Stuttgart

Port
Jackson
shark

Pair of starry
smooth-hounds

Fossil of
Ptychodus
tooth

Leopard shark

DK

A DORLING KINDERSLEY BOOK

Project editor Marion Dent
Art editor Jill Plank
Managing editor Helen Parker
Managing art editor Julia Harris
Production Louise Barratt
Picture research Suzanne Williams
Special photography Frank Greenaway, Dave King
Editorial consultant Dr Geoffrey Waller
Model makers Graham High, Jeremy Hunt
Special thanks Sea Life Centres (UK)

Long spear for
catching sharks,
Nicobar Islands, India

This Eyewitness ® Guide has been conceived by
Dorling Kindersley Limited
and Editions Gallimard

Shark rattle,
Samoa, South
Pacific

Ray-skin-
covered
scabbard used
by Ashanti
tribe, Ghana,
West Africa

First published in Great Britain in 1992 by
Dorling Kindersley Limited,
9 Henrietta Street, London WC2E 8PS

Copyright © 1992 Dorling Kindersley Limited,
London

A CIP catalogue record for this book is available
from the British Library

ISBN 0 86318 912 1

Colour reproduction by Colourscan, Singapore
Printed in Singapore by Toppan

Contents

Model of a great white shark

What is a shark?

MANY PEOPLE THINK of sharks as mean and menacing with their pointed snouts, fearsome teeth, and staring eyes. Sharks are skilful predators, but only a few are a danger to people. The 375 or so species of shark range in size from a lantern shark at about 20 cm (8 in) long to the whale shark at over 12 m (40 ft) long, but half the species are less than 1 m (3.3 ft) long. Not all sharks are as streamlined as this spinner shark. Angel sharks have flattened bodies, horn sharks are blunt-headed, while bamboo sharks are long and flexible. All sharks belong to one class of fish called Chondrichthyes, having skeletons made of gristle-like cartilage. Sharks live in the sea, though a few live in or swim into inland waters.

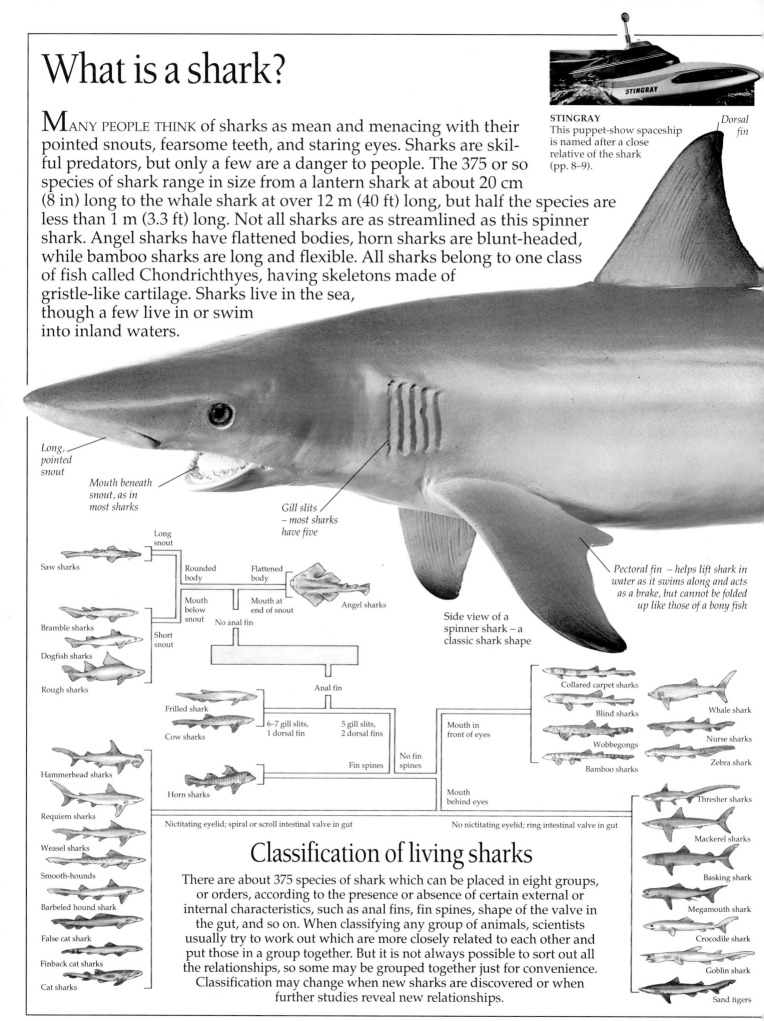

STINGRAY
This puppet-show spaceship is named after a close relative of the shark (pp. 8–9).

Dorsal fin

Long, pointed snout

Mouth beneath snout, as in most sharks

Gill slits – most sharks have five

Pectoral fin – helps lift shark in water as it swims along and acts as a brake, but cannot be folded up like those of a bony fish

Side view of a spinner shark – a classic shark shape

Saw sharks

Long snout

Rounded body

Flattened body

Mouth below snout

Mouth at end of snout

Angel sharks

Bramble sharks

Short snout

Dogfish sharks

Rough sharks

No anal fin

Frilled shark

Cow sharks

Anal fin

6–7 gill slits, 1 dorsal fin

5 gill slits, 2 dorsal fins

Hammerhead sharks

Horn sharks

Fin spines

No fin spines

Mouth in front of eyes

Collared carpet sharks

Blind sharks

Wobbegongs

Bamboo sharks

Whale shark

Nurse sharks

Zebra shark

Requiem sharks

Weasel sharks

Smooth-hounds

Barbeled hound shark

False cat shark

Finback cat sharks

Cat sharks

Mouth behind eyes

Nictitating eyelid; spiral or scroll intestinal valve in gut

No nictitating eyelid; ring intestinal valve in gut

Thresher sharks

Mackerel sharks

Basking shark

Megamouth shark

Crocodile shark

Goblin shark

Sand tigers

Classification of living sharks

There are about 375 species of shark which can be placed in eight groups, or orders, according to the presence or absence of certain external or internal characteristics, such as anal fins, fin spines, shape of the valve in the gut, and so on. When classifying any group of animals, scientists usually try to work out which are more closely related to each other and put those in a group together. But it is not always possible to sort out all the relationships, so some may be grouped together just for convenience. Classification may change when new sharks are discovered or when further studies reveal new relationships.

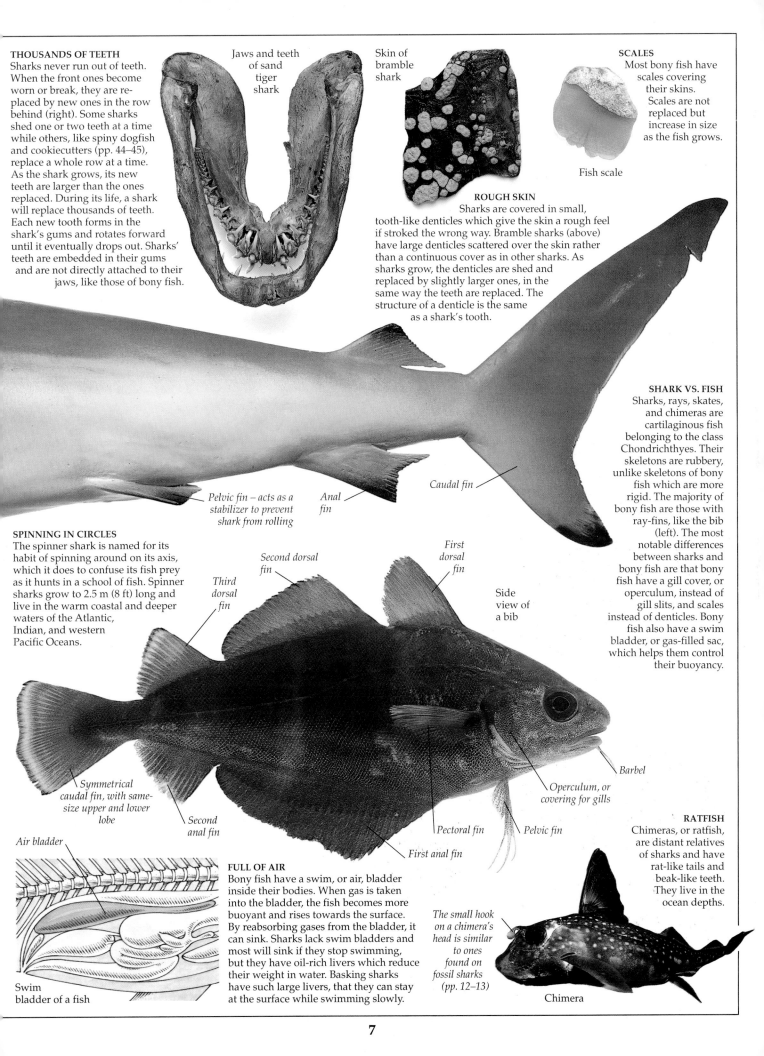

THOUSANDS OF TEETH
Sharks never run out of teeth. When the front ones become worn or break, they are replaced by new ones in the row behind (right). Some sharks shed one or two teeth at a time while others, like spiny dogfish and cookiecutters (pp. 44–45), replace a whole row at a time. As the shark grows, its new teeth are larger than the ones replaced. During its life, a shark will replace thousands of teeth. Each new tooth forms in the shark's gums and rotates forward until it eventually drops out. Sharks' teeth are embedded in their gums and are not directly attached to their jaws, like those of bony fish.

Jaws and teeth of sand tiger shark

Skin of bramble shark

SCALES
Most bony fish have scales covering their skins. Scales are not replaced but increase in size as the fish grows.

Fish scale

ROUGH SKIN
Sharks are covered in small, tooth-like denticles which give the skin a rough feel if stroked the wrong way. Bramble sharks (above) have large denticles scattered over the skin rather than a continuous cover as in other sharks. As sharks grow, the denticles are shed and replaced by slightly larger ones, in the same way the teeth are replaced. The structure of a denticle is the same as a shark's tooth.

SHARK VS. FISH
Sharks, rays, skates, and chimeras are cartilaginous fish belonging to the class Chondrichthyes. Their skeletons are rubbery, unlike skeletons of bony fish which are more rigid. The majority of bony fish are those with ray-fins, like the bib (left). The most notable differences between sharks and bony fish are that bony fish have a gill cover, or operculum, instead of gill slits, and scales instead of denticles. Bony fish also have a swim bladder, or gas-filled sac, which helps them control their buoyancy.

Pelvic fin – acts as a stabilizer to prevent shark from rolling

Anal fin

Caudal fin

SPINNING IN CIRCLES
The spinner shark is named for its habit of spinning around on its axis, which it does to confuse its fish prey as it hunts in a school of fish. Spinner sharks grow to 2.5 m (8 ft) long and live in the warm coastal and deeper waters of the Atlantic, Indian, and western Pacific Oceans.

Third dorsal fin

Second dorsal fin

First dorsal fin

Second view of a bib

Side view of a bib

Symmetrical caudal fin, with same-size upper and lower lobe

Second anal fin

Barbel

Operculum, or covering for gills

Pectoral fin

Pelvic fin

First anal fin

RATFISH
Chimeras, or ratfish, are distant relatives of sharks and have rat-like tails and beak-like teeth. They live in the ocean depths.

Air bladder

FULL OF AIR
Bony fish have a swim, or air, bladder inside their bodies. When gas is taken into the bladder, the fish becomes more buoyant and rises towards the surface. By reabsorbing gases from the bladder, it can sink. Sharks lack swim bladders and most will sink if they stop swimming, but they have oil-rich livers which reduce their weight in water. Basking sharks have such large livers, that they can stay at the surface while swimming slowly.

Swim bladder of a fish

The small hook on a chimera's head is similar to ones found on fossil sharks (pp. 12–13)

Chimera

Close relatives

A GRACEFUL MANTA RAY SWIMMING ALONG with slow beats of its huge wings looks nothing like a sleek reef shark. Yet rays and their cousins – skates, guitarfish, and sawfish – all belong to the same group as sharks called elasmobranchs. Members of this group have cartilaginous skeletons, which are flexible like rubber, and gill slits, instead of the flap-like opercula, or gill covers, found in bony fish and chimeras (pp. 6–7). All rays have wing-like pectoral fins joined to their heads, and gill slits on the undersides of their bodies. Most rays live on the sea bed where they feed on shellfish, worms, and fish.

THE MIGHTY MANTA
Manta rays, or devilfish, have enormous pectoral fins (wings), and measure up to 7 m (23 ft) across. This magnificent female specimen, caught off the New Jersey coast in the USA, weighed over 1300 kg (2860 lb). These harmless filter feeders use the large lobes on their heads to channel plankton into their wide mouths.

Starry ray

Spines increase in size along body from minute at snout to larger at tip of tail

Blonde ray

SPOT THE DIFFERENCE
Rays have a great variety of patterns on their upper sides which help to camouflage them while they rest on the sea bed. The spots on the blonde ray go right to the edge of its pectoral fins, while those on the spotted ray do not. The undersides of rays are usually white.

Spotted ray

Second dorsal fin

First dorsal fin

Painted ray

Spines along back for extra protection against predators

Guitarfish

RAY OR SKATE?
Thornback ray is often sold as edible skate, but common skate actually grows to twice the thornback's size, reaching 2 m (6.5 ft) long.

BABY RAY
This one-month-old spotted baby ray will take eight years before it matures and is able to reproduce.

STRANGE RAYS
Both guitarfish (50 species) and sawfish (six species) belong to the same group as rays. Guitarfish live mostly in warmer seas, while sawfish are also found in rivers and lakes. Sawfish look like saw sharks, but do not have their two long barbels in the middle of their "saws" and gill slits are on the undersides of their bodies, not on the sides of their heads, as in sharks. Sawfish and saw sharks use their saws for feeding and defence.

Sawfish

Pectoral fin

Eye

Spiracle – one-way valve to draw water in, which is then pumped out through gill slits underneath

Pelvic fin

Undulate ray

Sting

SWIMMING AROUND
Most rays swim by using their pectoral fins. But, electric rays, sawfish, and some species of guitarfish swim in the same way as sharks do, by sculling with their tails. This spotted ray's tail is too spindly to provide much propulsion, so undulations, or waves, pass down the length of the ray's pectoral fins from front to back. As they swim along they appear to fly through the water. The up-and-down motion of the pectoral fins, or wings, is shown much better in species with enormous wings, like the manta ray. These giant rays are even able to leap clear out of the water, sometimes up to 1.5 m (5 ft).

STINGRAY
There are over 160 different species of stingrays and they live all around the world, in both warm and cool waters. Most are armed with one, or sometimes several, venomous spines on their tails.

Typical swimming sequence of rays

Inside a shark

PACKAGED NEATLY INSIDE this spinner shark's body are all the organs that keep it alive. To breathe, sharks have gills which absorb oxygen from the water and release carbon dioxide back into it. These gases are transported to and from the gills by the blood. The heart pumps the blood around the body, delivering oxygen and nutrients while taking away carbon dioxide and other wastes. To get energy for all their activities, including growth and repair, sharks need to eat. Food passes into the digestive system, which is like a large tube. From the mouth the food goes down the gullet into the stomach, where digestion begins, and then into the intestine where digested food is absorbed. Indigestible wastes collect in the rectum to be passed out of the body. Digested food is further processed in the large liver which also increases the shark's buoyancy. Kidneys remove wastes from the blood and regulate blood concentration. Large muscles in the body wall keep the shark swimming while the skeleton and skin provide support. The brain coordinates the shark's actions with signals or instructions passed back and forth along the spinal cord. Finally, sharks like all animals cannot live forever and must reproduce to carry on the species. Female sharks produce eggs from their ovaries and males sperm from their testes. When sperm meets egg, a new life begins.

DANGER BELOW
Sharks have been known to attack people coming down into water, as this Australian parachutist will soon discover.

Paired kidneys regulate waste products to keep concentration of body fluids just above that of sea water, or sharks will dehydrate

Segmented swimming muscles contract alternately, sending a wave motion from head to tail

Model of a female spinner shark, showing internal anatomy

Vent between claspers for disposing of body wastes

Clasper (male reproductive organ)

Male shark

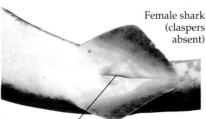

Female shark (claspers absent)

MALE OR FEMALE
All male sharks have a pair of claspers which are formed from the inner edge of their pelvic fins. During mating, one of the claspers is rotated forward and inserted into the female's body opening, or cloaca. Sperm is pumped down a groove in the clasper into the female, so fertilization of her eggs takes place inside her body.

Cloaca (opening for reproduction, and vent for waste disposal)

Rectal gland (third kidney) passes excess salt out of the body through the vent

ALL IN THE TAIL
Sharks have a backbone, or vertebral column, which extends into the upper lobe of their tail, or caudal fin. This type of caudal fin is called a heterocercal tail, as opposed to those in most bony fish where the upper lobe does not contain an extension of the vertebral column. Cartilaginous rods and dermal filaments help to strengthen the shark's tail.

Scroll valve in intestine, or gut – other sharks have spiral or ring valves

Left lobe of large liver

Caudal fin

Vertebral column

Cartilaginous rod

Dermal filament

BRAIN POWER

Some sharks have brains that are similar in weight to those of birds and mammals, when compared to their overall body weight. The nasal sac, or sensory part of the nose, is close to the front part of the brain.

Nasal sac

Forebrain

Midbrain

Hindbrain

Brain of a lemon shark

Ovary (eggs visible within its wall). When ripe, eggs pass into a tube for fertilization

Gill arch with gill filaments, where respiration takes place

Cartilage support of gill arch, forming a hoop around the gullet

Jaw-opening muscle pulls jaws forward so teeth protrude

Nostril

Tongue is rigid, supported by a pad of cartilage

Jaw-closing muscle

Cartilage in floor of gullet

Aorta, with branchial arteries

Heart

Open gill slits (below)

Shut gill slits (below)

BLOOD CIRCULATION

Blood from the body collects in the first chamber of the shark's heart, then is pumped through the second and third, while the fourth prevents blood flowing back into the heart. The aorta and branchial arteries circulate blood to the gills, where each branchial artery divides into tiny blood vessels in the gill filaments. As sea water passes over the gills, oxygen is picked up and carbon dioxide released.

Cartilage at base of pectoral fin

Cartilage of pectoral girdle supports pectoral fins and protects heart

Gall bladder

Pectoral fin

Second dorsal fin

FOOD PROCESSOR

Food begins its digestion process in the shark's stomach, then passes into the intestine, where the multi-layered scroll valve increases the area for absorbing digested food. A greeny-yellowy fluid, stored in the gall bladder, is released into the gut, where it helps fats be absorbed. The shark's large liver also aids digestion, processing fats, carbohydrates, and proteins.

First dorsal fin

Stomach's descending limb

OPEN, SHUT

To breathe, water comes in through the shark's mouth, passes over the gills, and out the gill slits. A nurse shark pumps water across its gills, by closing its mouth and contracting the mouth and gullet walls. When the mouth opens, the gill slits shut, when the mouth closes, the gill slits open.

Anal fin

Rear view of whole body of shark, showing gullet

Pelvic fin

Stomach's ascending limb

Spleen, producing red blood cells

Pancreas, producing enzymes to help digest food in gut

Ancient sharks

A megalodon's tooth (actual size)

Serrated edge for cutting

Actual size tooth of a great white shark (pp. 28–31)

Flat, ridged side for crushing prey

Tooth of *Ptychodus*

THE FIRST SHARKS appeared in the ancient seas 400 million years ago, about 200 million years before dinosaurs roamed the Earth. At that time there were no reptiles, birds, or mammals. The remains of some of these early sharks were fossilized when they fell to the bottom of the sea and became covered with layers of sand and other sediment. Hard parts, like spines and teeth, fossilized more easily than soft parts, which often rotted away. Sometimes all that is left are impressions of the sharks in rocks. Fossil shark teeth are common because these ancient sharks, like their living descendants, shed many teeth in a lifetime. Sharks' rubbery skeletons, made of cartilage, did not preserve as well as the hard skeletons of bony fish. Shark fossils are often discovered in rocks on land which, in prehistoric times, were under the sea. Scientists can tell how old fossils are from the age of the rocks in which they are found. The earliest groups of sharks became extinct, but the descendants of some groups that first appeared about 200 million years ago – like the bullheads (pp. 40–41), cat sharks, and cow sharks – are alive today.

WHAT BIG TEETH!
Shown above is a fossil tooth of a megalodon, or great tooth shark, compared to one from its living relative, the great white shark. Megalodons reached 13 m (43 ft) long and must have been formidable predators when they cruised the seas about 15 million years ago. A megalodon probably used its teeth for slashing deep into large prey, as great whites do today. The small, ridged tooth is from *Ptychodus* from 120 million years ago. These sharks probably ate shellfish, crushing them against the hard tooth ridges. They died out at the same time as the dinosaurs, about 65 million years ago.

JUST A JUVENILE
Looking much the same as its living relative – the lesser spotted dogfish (pp. 20–21) – this young shark died at least 65 million years ago. It is preserved in a piece of rock from the Lebanon in the Middle East.

Caudal fin like a mako's – upper lobe strengthened by extended vertebral column, like all sharks

Second dorsal fin would have had a short spine in front

Relatively small dorsal fin, also had a spine in front

CLADOSELACHE
This model reveals what *Cladoselache*, one of the earliest known sharks, probably looked like. Almost 2 m (6.6 ft) long, this shark swam in the ancient seas about 360 million years ago. It had a powerful tail, like a mako shark (pp. 16–17), so it could probably swim quite fast, but the pectoral fins were broader than those of fast, modern sharks, possibly making it a less agile swimmer. *Cladoselache* could swim well enough to catch fish, some of which have even been preserved in the stomachs of fossils. Unlike many modern sharks, *Cladoselache's* mouth was at the tip of its snout.

Small, broad-based, triangular pelvic fin in this model projects horizontally

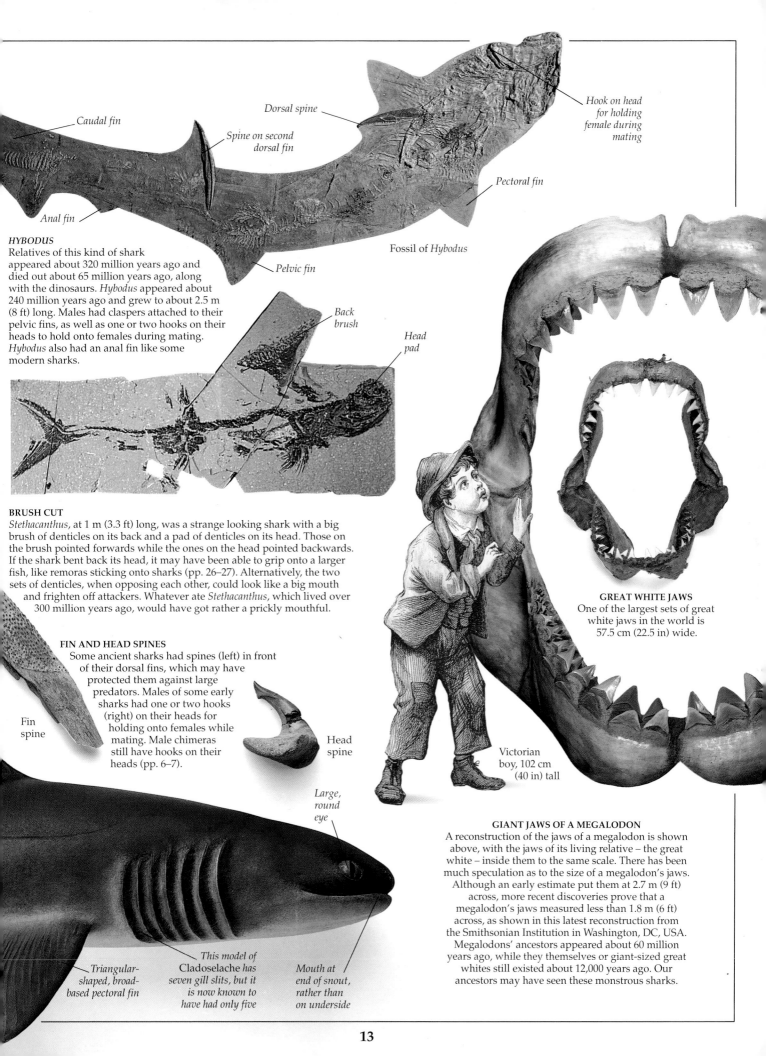

Caudal fin

Dorsal spine

Hook on head
for holding
female during
mating

Spine on second
dorsal fin

Pectoral fin

Fossil of *Hybodus*

Anal fin

HYBODUS
Relatives of this kind of shark
appeared about 320 million years ago and
died out about 65 million years ago, along
with the dinosaurs. *Hybodus* appeared about
240 million years ago and grew to about 2.5 m
(8 ft) long. Males had claspers attached to their
pelvic fins, as well as one or two hooks on their
heads to hold onto females during mating.
Hybodus also had an anal fin like some
modern sharks.

Pelvic fin

Back
brush

Head
pad

BRUSH CUT
Stethacanthus, at 1 m (3.3 ft) long, was a strange looking shark with a big
brush of denticles on its back and a pad of denticles on its head. Those on
the brush pointed forwards while the ones on the head pointed backwards.
If the shark bent back its head, it may have been able to grip onto a larger
fish, like remoras sticking onto sharks (pp. 26–27). Alternatively, the two
sets of denticles, when opposing each other, could look like a big mouth
and frighten off attackers. Whatever ate *Stethacanthus*, which lived over
300 million years ago, would have got rather a prickly mouthful.

FIN AND HEAD SPINES
Some ancient sharks had spines (left) in front
of their dorsal fins, which may have
protected them against large
predators. Males of some early
sharks had one or two hooks
(right) on their heads for
holding onto females while
mating. Male chimeras
still have hooks on their
heads (pp. 6–7).

Fin
spine

Head
spine

GREAT WHITE JAWS
One of the largest sets of great
white jaws in the world is
57.5 cm (22.5 in) wide.

Victorian
boy, 102 cm
(40 in) tall

Large,
round
eye

GIANT JAWS OF A MEGALODON
A reconstruction of the jaws of a megalodon is shown
above, with the jaws of its living relative – the great
white – inside them to the same scale. There has been
much speculation as to the size of a megalodon's jaws.
Although an early estimate put them at 2.7 m (9 ft)
across, more recent discoveries prove that a
megalodon's jaws measured less than 1.8 m (6 ft)
across, as shown in this latest reconstruction from
the Smithsonian Institution in Washington, DC, USA.
Megalodons' ancestors appeared about 60 million
years ago, while they themselves or giant-sized great
whites still existed about 12,000 years ago. Our
ancestors may have seen these monstrous sharks.

Triangular-
shaped, broad-
based pectoral fin

This model of
Cladoselache has
seven gill slits, but it
is now known to
have had only five

Mouth at
end of snout,
rather than
on underside

Amazing grace

Sharks are graceful swimmers propelling themselves through the water by beating their tails from side to side. The pectoral fins are held out from the body and as water flows over them, lift is generated to keep the shark from sinking. Further lift is produced by the upper lobe of the tail, which tends to push the head down, so that the shark can swim on the level. Shark fins are not nearly as flexible as those of bony fish, but adjustments to the angle at which the fins are held, control whether the shark goes up, down, left, or right. Pectoral fins are also used for braking. Some sharks that live on the sea bed, such as horn sharks (pp. 40–41) and epaulette sharks, can use their pectoral fins to crawl along the bottom. Unlike bony fish, sharks cannot move their pectoral fins like paddles so are unable to swim backwards or hover in the water. They also lack swim bladders which act as buoyancy aids in bony fish. However, they do have oil-rich livers (pp. 10–11) which help reduce their weight in water.

THE THREE GRACES
According to Greek mythology, these three daughters of Zeus were the goddesses of grace and beauty.

TAIL END
Undulations, or "S"-shaped waves, pass down a shark's body, as it moves forward (above). The tail bends more than the rest of the body, producing a forward thrust.

STARRY SMOOTH-HOUND
The denticles on a shark's skin line up with the direction of travel, helping to reduce drag (resistance to water). These denticles may trap a film of water, helping sharks move through it more easily.

CRUISING
With pectoral fins held straight out from its sides, the starry smooth-hound (right) keeps swimming at the same level. The two dorsal fins stop the shark rolling and its tail gives a forward thrust.

14

One-year-old
leopard shark,
38 cm (15 in) long

SEE HOW IT BENDS
Leopard sharks (above) have flexible
bodies, so they can turn around
in small spaces. Like their close
relatives, the smooth-hounds, leopard
sharks spend much of their time cruising
close to the bottom and also rest on the sea bed.

IN FLIGHT
The large pectoral fins of the starry smooth-hound (left) are
similar to an aeroplane's wings because they provide lift to keep the
shark from sinking. When tilted they can also act as brakes like the flaps
on the wings of an aeroplane which are raised on landing. Submarines
have horizontal fins, called hydrofoils, which lift them upwards like
those of a shark. Just like hydrofoils, the leading (or front) edge of a
shark's pectoral fins is rounded and the trailing (or rear) edge is thin,
so that water flows over them more easily. The pointed snout and
tapered body are streamlined to give less resistance to water.

FULL STEAM AHEAD
A great white shark
(above) normally
cruises at about 3 kph
(1.8 mph). Its bulky
body hardly moves at
all, while its tail beats
from side to side.
When closing in on
a kill, the great white
puts on an impressive
burst of speed of up
to 25 kph (15 mph).

ON THE TURN
Great whites can bend
their bodies but are not
nearly as flexible as
smaller sharks. They
have to surprise their
prey rather than out-
manoeuvring them.

Continued on next page

Continued from previous page

Tails and more tails

The shape of a shark's tail suits its lifestyle. Many sharks have tail fins where the upper lobe is larger than the lower, and as the tail swings from side to side, this lobe produces lift which tends to push the head down. This is compensated by lift from the pectoral fins, which stops the shark from sinking to the bottom. In fast sharks, like the mako and great white, these two lobes are almost equal in size. Lift may also come from the base of the tail which, in the mako, has small, horizontal keels. The extra height of these more symmetrical-shaped tails gives a more powerful thrust. Slow bottom-dwellers, like the nurse, have less powerful tails and their swimming motion is more eel-like, with obvious waves passing down to their tails.

BONNETHEAD'S TAIL
Bonnetheads are small hammer-heads (pp. 42–43), which grow to about 1.5 m (5 ft) in length. Like all sharks, the tail's upper lobe contains an extension of the vertebral column and is usually larger than the lower lobe. The upper lobe is held at an angle so it is raised above the shark's midline (imagine a line drawn through the shark from the tip of its snout to the end of its body).

Tail of a
bonnethead
shark

THRESHER'S TAIL
The upper lobe of the tail (left) of a thresher shark is as long as its body. From 1.5–2.5 m (5–8 ft) in length, the tails of the three different types of thresher (pp. 58–59) are by far the longest of any shark. The tail of a thresher is used to stun its prey and also can inflict nasty injuries on anglers when the sharks are hauled on board.

Tail of a
thresher
shark

Keel

GREAT WHITE'S TAIL
The upper and lower lobes of a great white's tail fin are almost equal in size. They lie high above, and low below, the shark's midline respectively. The keel helps the big shark to turn. The first dorsal fin is rigid and prevents the shark from rolling. Also a great white can jump out of the water.

Tail view of a model
of a great white shark
(pp. 28–29)

ANGEL GETS GOING

To lift its huge body off the sea bed, the angel shark beats its tail back and forth while tipping its large pectoral and pelvic fins for maximum lift. Once off the sea bed, angels propel themselves forward by sculling with their tails, but they do not undulate, or wave, their pectoral fins like rays.

MID-AIR MAKO

Makos (pp. 26–27) are probably the fastest sharks in the sea, reaching speeds estimated to be 32 kph (19 mph) for a few moments. When caught on an angler's line, they leap clear of the surface in an effort to escape (above). Their tails are the same shape as another fast fish, the tuna, and like them they have keels along the base of their tails which may give them more manoeuvrability and perhaps provide some lift. They are active predators, pursuing mainly fish.

Lower lobe of angel shark's tail fin (pp. 36–37) is longer than upper lobe

SWELL SHARK'S TAIL

Smaller than nurse sharks, at 1 m (3.3 ft) long, swell sharks (right) are sluggish animals, spending the day resting on the sea bed and at night swimming close to the bottom. Their tails are barely held above their midlines.

HORN SHARK'S TAIL

The lower lobe of the horn shark's tail (pp. 40–41) is more developed than the swell shark's. The tail of this 1-m (3.3-ft) long shark (right) is still held at a low angle to its midline and it is a slow swimmer.

TAIL OF A NURSE SHARK

Nurse sharks, at 3 m (10 ft) long, are rather slow swimmers and use their tails (right) for cruising close to the bottom.

Making sense

Blue shark's nictitating eyelid

Pore

Nostril

SHARKS HAVE THE SAME FIVE SENSES as people – they can see, hear, smell, taste, and touch. There is also a sixth sense which allows sharks to detect weak, electrical signals generated by their prey. This electro-sense may also help them to navigate on their journeys in the sea. This under-water world is quite different to our own. Light levels decrease with depth and colours fade to blues. Sound travels five times faster and farther. Odours are dissolved in water, not wafted in the air. Sharks can detect vibrations made by animals moving through the water, giving them the sense called "distant-touch". It is hard to find out exactly how a shark perceives its world, but studies on their behaviour and how sense organs work give some idea about what it is like to be a shark.

METAL DETECTOR
Sweeping a metal detector back and forth to find buried metal objects is like the way hammerheads (pp. 42–43) hunt for fish hiding in the sand.

GOING TO ITS HEAD
Like us, a shark's major sense organs are on its head. Seen on this blue shark are the eye, nostril, and sensory pores, which detect weak electric signals. The eye is partly covered by a third eyelid, called a nictitating (or blinking) eyelid, which protects the eye when the shark attacks its prey or nears unfamiliar objects. As the shark swims along, water flows through the nostril beneath the tip of the snout, bringing a constant stream of odours.

FEEDING FRENZY
When sharks are feeding on baits, they may become over-excited and snap wildly at their food. They may bite each other and even tear one another apart.

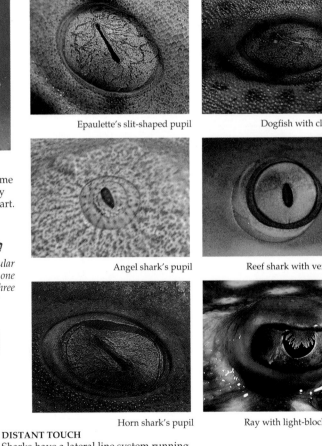

Epaulette's slit-shaped pupil

Dogfish with closed pupil

Angel shark's pupil

Reef shark with vertical pupil

Horn shark's pupil

Ray with light-blocking screen

Semi-circular canal, one of three

THE INNER EAR
Sharks do not have external ear flaps, but have ears inside their heads on either side of the brain case. Three semi-circular canals placed at right angles to each other are like those found in the ears of all vertebrates. These canals help a shark work out which way it has turned in the water. Receptors in the inner ear, like those in the lateral line on the skin, pick up sounds travelling through the water. Each ear has a small duct which leads to a pore on the top of the shark's head.

ALL KINDS OF EYES
According to how much light there is, the iris in a shark's eyes contracts or expands to alter the size of the pupil. A layer of cells at the back of the eye, called the tapetum, reflects light back onto the retina where images are focused, making maximum use of any available light. This helps sharks to see in dim light. Cats also have a tapetum which is why their eyes reflect lights shone at them. On bright sunny days a shark can shield its tapetum with a layer of pigment. Like humans a shark's retina has two types of cells – rods work in dim light and are sensitive to light changes; cones resolve details and probably allow sharks to see in colour.

DISTANT TOUCH
Sharks have a lateral line system running down each side of the body and onto its head. The lines are small canals with tiny pores beneath which are cells with minute hairs. Scattered over the body are similar hair cells called pit organs, which like the lateral lines pick up vibrations.

Lateral line

Starry smooth-hound showing lateral line

EYES ON STALKS
Hammerheads' eyes are on the end of their head projections, giving them a good view as they swing their heads back and forth. The nostrils are widely spaced on the front of the head, helping them detect where an odour is coming from. The head projections are packed with ampullae of Lorenzini which detect electric signals from hidden fish.

Compass

Imaginary magnet

North-south axis

Earth's magnetic field

COMPASS SENSE
Some sharks migrate hundreds of kilometres and they seem to know where they are going, in what to us is a featureless ocean. Scientists think sharks have compass sense to guide them. In a real compass, a magnetic needle swings around to align itself to the Earth's magnetic field. The Earth's magnetic field (above) is created by its core, which acts like a giant magnet. Sharks seem able to swim in one direction by sensing changes in their own electric fields in relation to the Earth's magnetic field. Corrections have to be made for speed and direction of ocean currents, which may sweep the shark off course. Sharks may also be able to navigate by detecting magnetic patterns on the sea bed.

DUCK-BILLED PLATYPUS
One of the few animals, apart from sharks, which has a sixth sense of being able to detect electric signals of its prey, is the duck-billed platypus from Australia. The platypus's electro-receptors are on the left-hand side of its bill. Platypuses live in streams where they hunt for insects and other small creatures on the bottom.

Nurse shark

Barbel

FEELERS AND TASTE BUMPS
The pair of feelers, or barbels, on the nurse shark's nose (right) means it can feel prey such as shrimps hiding in the sand. Many of the sharks that live on the sea bed have barbels which they use to probe the sand for food. Barbels may also play a role in taste. Sharks have taste buds on bumps in their mouths and gullets (left). They spit out anything, if they do not like the taste.

Nostril

SPOTTY NOSE
The spots in front of the nostrils on this sand tiger's snout are sensory pores, called ampullae of Lorenzini. Full of jelly, the deep pores connect at their base to nerves. The pores detect the weak electric signals produced by their prey's muscles and bodily processes. Sometimes sharks are confused by electric signals given off by metal, so they will bite shark cages (pp. 52–53).

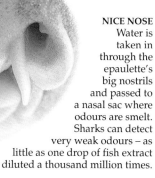

Snout of an epaulette shark

NICE NOSE
Water is taken in through the epaulette's big nostrils and passed to a nasal sac where odours are smelt. Sharks can detect very weak odours – as little as one drop of fish extract diluted a thousand million times.

19

Laying eggs

FINDING A MATE, for some sharks, means a long swim because males and females live in different parts of the ocean. When they meet, the male chases the female, biting her to encourage her to mate. He inserts one of his claspers into her cloaca, or body opening. Sea water already drawn into a sac in the male's body is then squirted into a groove in his clasper (pp. 10–11) to flush sperm into her cloaca. In this way, the sperm fertilizes the female's eggs inside her body, unlike bony fish, where fertilization occurs outside the body with sperm and eggs being shed into the water. Fertilization may not happen immediately because some female sharks can store sperm until they are ready to reproduce. In most sharks, fertilized eggs develop in the female's uterus, or egg tubes, and she gives birth to baby sharks, called pups (pp. 22–23). In other sharks, the fertilized eggs are encased in a leathery shell and deposited by the female on the sea bed. Once the eggs are laid, the female swims away, leaving them to develop and hatch on their own. These sharks are oviparous, which means their young hatch from an egg laid outside the mother – just like birds or bony fish.

MERMAIDS
Mermaids are mythical sea creatures with a woman's body and a fish's tail. Since ancient times, sailors have made up stories about mermaids. The empty egg cases of dogfish and rays that wash up on the seashore are called mermaids' purses.

CATCH ME IF YOU CAN
This male white tip reef shark is pursuing a female in the hope that she will mate with him. He may be attracted by her smell.

SPIRAL EGG
A horn shark wedges its spiral-shaped egg case into rocks to stop predators eating it.

CAT'S EGG
The cat shark's egg case is firmly anchored onto anything growing on the sea bed. Shark eggs are large and well protected and so stand a better chance of survival, compared to the masses of small eggs laid by bony fish.

LOVE BITES
When a male white tip reef shark gets close to a female (right), he bites her to arouse her interest in him. He will also grab her pectoral fin in his jaws to keep her close to him during mating. Very little is known of the mating habits of other large sharks.

THICK SKINS
Some female sharks, like this blue shark, have much thicker skins than males, so preventing serious injury during courtship. Most love bites are only skin deep and heal in a few weeks.

MATING SHARKS
People rarely see sharks mating in the wild, or even in aquariums. From a few observations, it seems that larger sharks mate side to side. White tip reef sharks (left) mate side to side and may pivot on their heads. The male of smaller sharks, such as dogfish (or cat sharks), is more flexible and wraps himself around the female when mating.

Tendril

DOGFISH EGGS
Baby dogfish, or embryos, lie safe inside their egg cases. Every year lesser spotted female dogfish, or small spotted cat sharks, lay about 20 eggs in seaweed. At first the egg cases are soft, but soon they harden in the sea water. The tendrils at the corners of the egg capsules anchor them onto seaweed to prevent them being swept away by currents. In the cool seas around the UK, embryos take about nine months to develop before they hatch. During this time each embryo gets its nourishment from its large yolk sac.

Dogfish embryo

Yolk sac

Pair of ten-day-old dogfish

Pair of dogfish egg cases

JUVENILE DOGFISH
These young dogfish are only ten days' old. Although they are only 10 cm (4 in) long, they look like small versions of their parents. Shark pups are generally much larger and more developed than fry of bony fish. Soon after hatching, the young dogfish start to feed on small creatures like shrimps. It will be ten years before they reach maturity and start to breed. When fully grown, dogfish are nearly 1 m (3.3 ft) long.

Cream-coloured underside

1 ONE-MONTH-OLD SWELL SHARK EMBRYO
Swell sharks live on the eastern side of the Pacific Ocean in shallow coastal waters. They are called swell sharks because when threatened they wedge themselves into a rocky crevice by gulping in mouthfuls of water. If taken out of the water, a swell shark can still swell up by taking in air. The female lays two eggs at a time, depositing them among clumps of seaweed. Each egg is protected by a leathery case. One month after it was laid, the fertilized egg has developed into a tiny embryo. A large egg sac is full of yolk which nourishes the growing embryo.

Colouring consists of light and dark brown bands, with dark spots on shark's top side

2 EMBRYO AT THREE MONTHS OF AGE
The embryo has grown much larger and it already has eyes and a tail. The yolk sac is connected to the embryo's belly by a cord, while oxygen in the surrounding sea water passes through the leathery egg case so that the embryo is able to breathe.

3 SEVEN-MONTH-OLD EMBRYO
By now the embryo looks much more like a baby shark. It has a complete set of fins and is able to wriggle about inside the egg case. The two rows of spines on the baby's back will help give it a grip on the egg case as it pushes its way out. The baby shark, or pup, will hatch as soon as it has used up the rest of the yolk sac.

Two-month-old swell shark pup

4 TWO-MONTH-OLD PUP
After ten months, the young swell shark – at 15 cm (6 in) long – has hatched from the egg case. This is a most vulnerable moment in its young life, as there are many predators around. The juvenile's mottled colour pattern makes it hard to see where it is hiding on the sea bed. It can also wedge itself into its hiding place by swelling up.

Live young

THE MAJORITY OF SHARKS give birth to live young instead of laying eggs. Most are ovoviviparous, producing large yolky eggs which are kept inside the mother's uterus. The developing pup, or embryo, is fed by the yolk sac attached to its belly. When this is used up, the pup is fully developed and ready to be born. In some shark species, the first pups that develop eat eggs and also embryos in their mother's uterus. In sand tiger (pp. 24–25) and mako sharks, only one of the young cannibals survives in each side of the paired uteri, having eaten all its unborn brothers and sisters. A more complex pregnancy occurs in a few viviparous sharks, such as lemon (pp. 54–55), blue, and bull, as well as hammerhead (pp. 42–43) sharks, in which nourishment from the mother's blood passes through the placenta to the embryo via the umbilical cord. This is also how human babies develop, as well as other placental mammals, such as dogs and elephants.

MOTHER AND BABY
Human babies need to be looked after for many years, but shark pups are not so lucky. They must fend for themselves as soon as they are born.

1

HOW A LEMON SHARK IS BORN
(1) The tip of the pup's tail is just visible poking out of its mother's opening, or cloaca (pp. 10–11). Pregnant lemon sharks come into shallow coastal lagoons which are sheltered from the waves, to give birth. Scientists studying sharks at Bimini in the Bahamas some- times catch female sharks for their investigations. (2) Here, the female has begun to give birth. (3) The scientist is acting like a midwife, and is helping the passage of the pup out of the mother's birth canal.

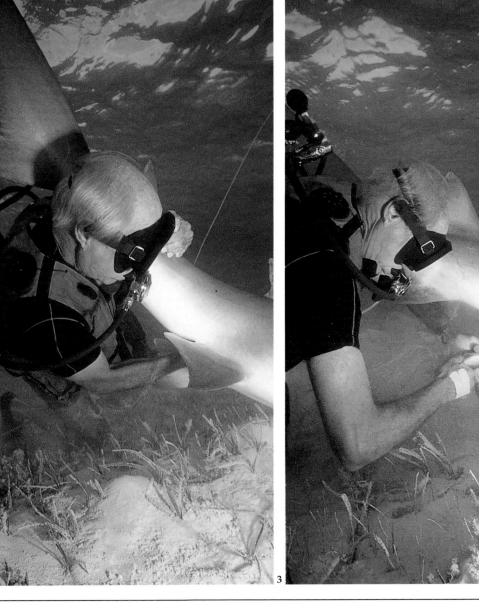

2   **3**

HAMMERHEAD PUPS

Hammerhead sharks give birth to live young that are little replicas of their parents. In one litter, up to 40 pups may be born, with their head projections bent back. In the uterus, each pup is connected to its mother by an umbilical cord.

BABY AFRICAN ELEPHANT

A baby elephant takes 22 months to develop inside its mother's womb, which is the longest gestation period of any mammal. Such a long period is not surprising since a baby elephant weighs over 100 kg (220 lb) at birth. Some sharks have a nine-month gestation period, just like humans, although the spiny dogfish matches the elephant in taking 18 to 24 months to be born.

SPINY BABIES DO NOT HURT THEIR MOTHERS

Pushing a baby out of the birth canal is hard for any mother. At least the spines of hedgehog babies do not poke out through their skin until after they are born. The sharp spines on the dorsal fins of baby spiny dogfish have protective coverings.

BIGEYE THRESHER PUPS

As bigeye thresher pups develop inside the uterus, they feed on bundles of un-fertilized eggs. The pups have long tails – just like their parents.

(4) The lemon shark pup, one of up to 17 pups, is still attached to its mother by the umbilical cord. She is nearly 3 m (10 ft) long, but her pups are only 60 cm (24 in) long. (5) The pup will rest for a while on the sea bed, then swims away, breaking the umbilical cord. (6) Now the pup faces life on its own. It must seek the cover of mangrove roots and hide from predators, such as larger sharks and barracudas. For many years it will stay in a small nursery area in the shallows of the lagoon, near where it was born. Then it will make exploratory trips out of the lagoon to the coral reefs and will gradually spend more time further out to sea.

4

5

6

CLAWS

This 19-mm (0.75-in) long copepod digs its sharp claws into a basking shark's skin. It feeds on skin secretions and blood. Basking sharks, infested by these and other parasites, become irritated and may even leap clear of the water to get rid of them.

Claw
Antenna
Head
Thoracic plate, or body section
Abdomen

BARNACLES ABOARD

This strange looking lump is a barnacle, related to the ones found on the seashore. In the sea, the larvae, or young, of this barnacle attach themselves to dorsal fins of spurdogs or dogfish. The root, or stalk, of this 26-mm (1-in) long barnacle has rootlets which absorb nutrients from the shark.

Soft shell
Root
Rootlet for absorbing food from shark

Female   Male

CLING ONS

These small crustaceans, or copepods (13 mm, 0.5 in long), have adhesion pads to stick onto sharks' fins. They feed on skin secretions.

Friend or foe?

LIKE MOST ANIMALS, sharks have a variety of small friends and enemies which choose to live on or within them. Remoras benefit from sharks because they hitch a ride on them. They stick onto sharks using suckers on their heads, but they can also swim well on their own, as well as riding bow waves produced by a shark swimming though the water. Other kinds of fish, called pilot fish, also swim with sharks and ride their bow waves. Parasites harm sharks by feeding on their skin, blood, or even inside them. They may cause the shark discomfort, but parasites rarely kill the shark. Some parasites, like tapeworms, have complicated life cycles passing through several different animals before they can infect sharks.

CLEAN TEETH
Other animals have friends too. A bird cleans a crocodile's teeth and finds something tasty to eat.

STREAMERS

Copepods are clinging onto the dorsal fins of this mako shark (above) and have egg cases streaming out behind them. Each case contains a stack of disc-shaped eggs. When the eggs are released, they hatch into tiny young, or larvae. These larvae drift about in the sea, passing through several stages of development before attaching themselves to a passing shark.

STICKING TOGETHER

Shark suckers, or remoras (left), live in the world's tropical oceans. Each has a ridged sucker on the top of its head which it uses to attach itself to sharks and rays. While hitching a ride, remoras may do their hosts a favour by nibbling off skin parasites. They may also steal scraps when the shark has a meal and even feed on the placenta, or afterbirth, when a shark produces pups (above).

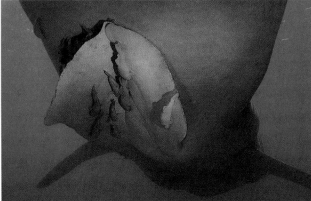

MOBILE HOME
Whale sharks (top) are so big that they provide living space for large numbers of remoras. Some remoras congregate around the mouth, even swimming inside the mouth cavity and gills where they may feed on parasites, while others nestle around the cloaca on a female shark (above). Remoras get free transport from their giant hosts, either by clinging on or riding the shark's bow wave.

WORMS AND MORE WORMS
Hundreds of 30-cm (1-ft) tapeworms may live in a shark's gut where, attached by spiny tentacles, they absorb food. Segments full of eggs from their tail ends are passed into the sea and the eggs hatch when eaten by a copepod. A young worm is passed on when a bony fish eats the copepod, and then a shark eats the fish.

Anchor which embeds in eye's surface

Arm

Head

Trunk

Egg sac, containing thousands of eggs

Tentacle

Head

Body

EYE SPY
This strange copepod hangs by its long arms to a Greenland shark's eye. At 31 mm (1.2 in) long, the parasite makes it hard for a 6-m (20-ft) length shark to see. It feeds on the eye's surface tissues, but once there, it cannot let go.

PILOT FISH
Young golden trevally from the Pacific Ocean swim with larger fish, including sharks. Though they are called pilot fish, they do not guide sharks and other large fish to sources of food, but just like to school with larger fish. Also they may gain protection because other fish do not like to be close to sharks. Pilot fish are much too agile to be eaten themselves.

NAVIGATING
A large ship is guided into harbour by pilot boats but sharks navigate on their own (pp. 18–19).

The great white shark

A POWERFUL PREDATOR, the great white inspires fear. This awesome shark grows to over 6 m (20 ft) long and weighs more than 2 tonnes (2.2 tons). It is the largest of the predatory sharks, capable of eating seals whole. The great white became famous in the *Jaws* movies where it appeared as a blood-thirsty creature intent on killing people. Attacks (pp. 48–49) on people are rare, and possibly occur when a shark mistakes a person for its usual seal prey. Despite its fame, little is known about the great white because it is rarely seen. Scientists have yet to discover where mating and birth occur, and their age when they reproduce or die. No-one knows how many great whites there are, but in some areas they may be on the decline.

FRENCH LANDING
This old engraving of a great white landed on France's Mediterranean coast shows how a century ago people were also fascinated by sharks. Unless they were lucky enough to see sharks first hand, artists had to rely on descriptions to make their drawings since there were no photographs. There are several inaccuracies in this engraving – the artist has given the great white the tail of a thresher and gill covers, like bony fish, as well as gill slits.

Dorsal fin

Small second dorsal fin, compared to size of first dorsal fin

Pelvic fin

Front view of model of a great white shark

Swimming keel

Long snout

Upper and lower lobes of caudal fin are almost symmetrical (pp. 16–17)

Relatively small anal fin

Clasper

WARM BLOOD
Great whites and their relatives – the mako, thresher, and porbeagle – are all warm-blooded, which means that they are able to keep their body temperature higher than the surrounding water. Only mammals, birds, and a few fast fish, like the tuna, are warm-blooded. These sharks have blood vessels in their muscles arranged in complex nets, so that the warm blood leaving the muscles passes heat to the cool blood coming from the gills (pp. 10–11). A high body temperature means that great whites have warm muscles which are able to act fast. This is important for a predator that has to make a high-speed dash to catch its prey. Being warm-blooded may also help the great white to digest its food more quickly. Scientists estimate that after a big feed a great white can last three months before needing another meal.

Pore marking position of ampullae of Lorenzini – sensory organs for detecting prey's electric field (pp. 18–19)

Long gill slit – one of five

Sharp, serrated teeth

WHITE DEATH
A great white's colouring makes it difficult to see in the water, so it is able to sneak up on its victims. When seen from below, a shark's white undersides blend in with a bright sky's reflection at the water's surface. This magnificent shark is sometimes called "white pointer", referring to its pointed snout which makes it more stream-lined. Great whites often have scratches and scars on their snouts which may be the result of their prey fighting back. They may also be bitten by larger members of their own kind which move in to take bait away from them.

Full-length side view of model of a male great white shark

Pectoral fin

TAKING THE BAIT
Scientists, film-makers, and photographers use chum (a mixture of blood and rotting fish) and baits to attract great whites. These are among the few sharks that stick their heads out of the water before and, sometimes, during attacks on prey. As the shark takes the bait, its eyes roll back in their sockets revealing the white surface of the eyeball. This protects the more vital front part of the eye from being scratched, which may happen if the shark was attacking live prey, such as a seal armed with claws and teeth.

TAGGING A GREAT WHITE
Dr. John McCosker, an American shark scientist, tags a great white off the Australian coast (top). Sonic tags have revealed that a great white can cruise at 3 kph (1.8 mph), travelling about 200 km (120 miles) in three days (above).

Continued on next page

Distribution of the great white shark

BIG BITE
A great white's upper jaw protrudes forward and its snout is tipped upward (right), so it can grab a chunk of meat. This shark may realize that there is no danger of its prey retaliating because the shark's eyes face forward and are not rolled back.

What a great white eats

Great white sharks live in the cool to warm waters along the coasts of the Americas, north and south Africa, the Mediterranean, Japan, China, Korea, Australia, and New Zealand. They also, occasionally, occur around some islands in the mid-Pacific and Atlantic Oceans. They are often seen near seal colonies, where they prey on both adults and young, but only a few sharks seem to hunt in any one area. When attacking a seal, a great white approaches unseen from below, takes a bite, then moves off for a short while. The prey soon weakens due to loss of blood and shock, so the shark can finish it off more easily. The great white's diet changes as it grows up. Young sharks of about 2–3 m (7–10 ft) long eat mostly fish, while older sharks around 4 m (13 ft) long tackle larger prey such as seals and sea lions.

ON THE MENU
Great whites eat a variety of animals including bony fish, other sharks, some sea birds, marine mammals (such as seals and porpoises), and, occasionally, people! Great whites are also scavengers and will eat whale carcasses and other dead animals. Unless a great white is seen feeding, it is hard to know if an animal found in its stomach had already died before it was eaten.

Diver for dinner

Leopard sharks (above) are eaten by young great whites along the Pacific coast of North America

TOP TIGER
Tigers and great whites are the top predators of land and sea, respectively. As adults, no other animals eat them though they are killed by people. However, tigers, like great whites, sometimes eat people.

Scientists have found remains of jackass penguins, from South Africa, with bite marks made by great whites

Bony fish, such as cabezon (above), are eaten by young great whites along the Pacific coast of North America

California sea lions (right) are eaten by adult great whites

Young elephant seals (above) are easy prey

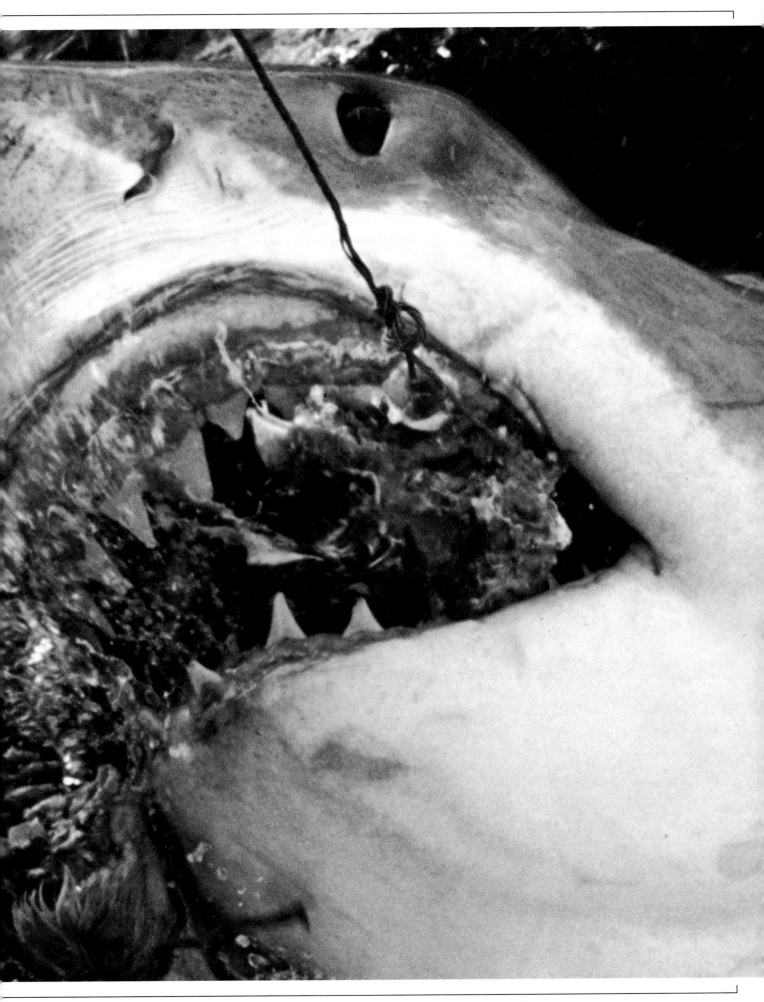

Gentle giants

HUMPBACK WHALES
Whale sharks are named after those other ocean giants – the whales – which are not fish but mammals.

WHALE SHARKS are the largest fish in the world, reaching at least 12 m (40 ft) long and weighing 13.2 tonnes (13 tons), about as large as an adult grey whale. These docile sharks are harmless and will allow scuba divers to take rides by hanging onto their fins – the only danger is getting scraped by their rough skin, or accidentally knocked by the huge tail as it swings back and forth. These giant fish can cruise at 3 kph (1.8 mph), often near the surface – being so large they have been run into by ships. They live in warm tropical waters in places where there is a good supply of food to support their large bulk, and feed by filtering food out of the water. Whale sharks may either lay enormous 30-cm (14-in) long eggs or give birth to live young, hatched from eggs inside their bodies (pp. 20–23).

NOT MUCH OF A BITE
Whale sharks do not bite or chew food, so they do not need their teeth which are no bigger than a match head.

Distribution of whale sharks

AT THE DENTIST
People use their teeth to chew food. If their teeth are removed, they need to be replaced by false ones.

A GREAT GULP
Despite their great size, whale sharks feed on plankton (small animals that drift in the sea), small fish and squid. Other large fish, such as basking sharks (pp. 34–35), manta rays (pp. 8–9), and baleen whales also feed by filtering food out of the water. Whale sharks scoop up water into their huge mouths and, as water passes over their gills and out through their gill slits, food is strained in filters attached to the gills. These filters are made up of a mesh of tissues supported by cartilaginous rods. Whale sharks occasionally eat larger fish such as mackerel and tuna, which are swallowed as they scoop up shoals of tiny fish. They can feed in a vertical position, even sticking their heads out of the water and sinking down to draw large fish into their mouths.

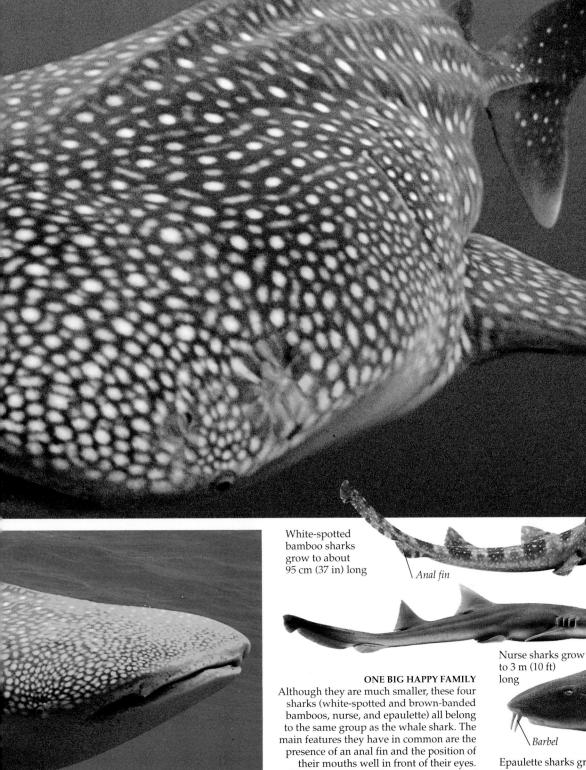

White-spotted
bamboo sharks
grow to about
95 cm (37 in) long

Anal fin

Brown-banded bamboo
sharks grow to just
over 1 m (3.3 ft)
long

Nurse sharks grow
to 3 m (10 ft)
long

Barbel

ONE BIG HAPPY FAMILY
Although they are much smaller, these four
sharks (white-spotted and brown-banded
bamboos, nurse, and epaulette) all belong
to the same group as the whale shark. The
main features they have in common are the
presence of an anal fin and the position of
their mouths well in front of their eyes.
They also have two barbels on the tips of
their snouts which help them find food.
Unlike the whale shark, these much
smaller sharks all live on the sea bed.

Epaulette sharks grow to just over 1 m (3.3 ft)
long

Basking beauties

CRUISING ALONG WITH THEIR HUGE MOUTHS wide open, basking sharks are like giant mobile sieves filtering out countless tiny creatures on which they feed. This shark is the second largest fish in the world, after the whale shark (pp. 32–33), growing to about 10 m (33 ft) long and weighing over 4 tonnes (3.9 tons). Basking sharks often swim at the surface on sunny days with their dorsal fins, and perhaps their snouts or tails out of the water. They are probably more attracted by a concentration of food at the surface than the delights of basking in the sunshine. Unfortunately, when the sharks are at the surface, they make easy targets for fishermen who harpoon them for the oil in their large livers which may be a quarter of their body weight. These sharks are also killed because of the damage they do to salmon nets. There is concern that too many are caught, as so little is known about their numbers, how far they travel, and how they reproduce (pp. 20–23).

SHARK FISHING
At Achill Island off Ireland's northwest coast, basking sharks were once netted in a bay, then speared with a lance, and dragged ashore. Fishing stopped when the numbers of sharks coming into the bay declined.

Eye

Nostril

Gill arch – water passes through arch and then through a sieve of gill rakers before flowing over the gills and out through the gill slits

OILY MOUTHS
Oil from sharks' livers has been used in cosmetics like lipsticks.

Nostril

Eye

Gill rakers

Open mouth of basking shark

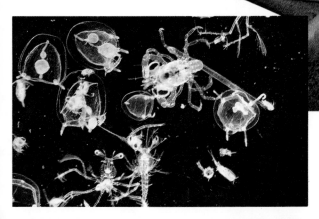

OPEN MOUTHED

As the basking shark swims along, one and a half million litres (330,000 gallons) of water flow through its huge mouth each hour. Drifting in the water are tiny creatures like baby crabs, fish eggs, copepods, and arrow worms – all known as plankton (left) – which are strained out of the water by hundreds of long bristles, or gill rakers (pp. 24–25), and trapped in a layer of slime. After a minute the basking shark closes its mouth, emptying the water out through its gill slits before swallowing its food. In winter, when plankton becomes scarce in the cool waters where basking sharks live, they stop feeding and shed their gill rakers. No-one knows where basking sharks go in winter, but they may sink to the bottom to rest on the sea bed. In spring, basking sharks appear on the water's surface where they start to feed again, having grown a new set of gill rakers.

Distribution of basking sharks

SHARKS AT WAR

In World War II some fighter planes used shark oil to lubricate their instruments. These American planes are decorated with shark jaws to frighten the enemy, but these painted sharks have much bigger teeth than basking sharks do.

Angel sharks

IMAGINE RUNNING A STEAM-ROLLER over a normal-shaped shark – the result would look rather like an angel shark. These strange, flattened sharks have extra-large pectoral fins resembling angels' wings. Angel sharks spend much of their lives resting on the sea bed or lying in wait for fish or shellfish to move within reach of their snapping, sharp-toothed jaws. They can also swim, using their tails to propel themselves along, just like other sharks. Angel sharks are most active between dusk and dawn, travelling as far as 9 km (5.5 miles) during the night. There are 13 species of angel shark that live in shallow coastal waters around the world to depths of over 1000 m (3300 ft).

MONK FISH
Ever since the 16th century, angel sharks have been called "monk fish", because the shape of their heads looks like the hood on a monk's cloak.

Distribution
of angel sharks

0   2000   4000   6000 km

Lower lobe of tail, or caudal fin, is longer than the upper lobe – a feature unique to angel sharks

Second dorsal fin

Pelvic fin

First dorsal fin

Gill slit

Mouth

Eye

Spiracle

Pelvic fin

LOOK-ALIKES
Rays (pp. 8–9) are flat, just like angel sharks. But unlike angel sharks, a ray's pectoral fins are completely attached to its head and its gill slits are located on the underside of its body.

Underside of ray

Pectoral fin

Top side of ray

ANGELS
This angel shark grows to nearly 2 m (6.5 ft) long. It is found in the Mediterranean and Baltic Seas, the eastern Atlantic Ocean, and the English Channel, down to depths of about 150 m (490 ft). Like all angel sharks, it has eyes on the top of its head so it can see while lying flat on the sea bed. For respiration, it can draw in water through its large spiracles, which are also placed on the top of its head. Water taken in through the spiracles is more likely to be free of silt, that could clog up its gills, than water taken in through its mouth.

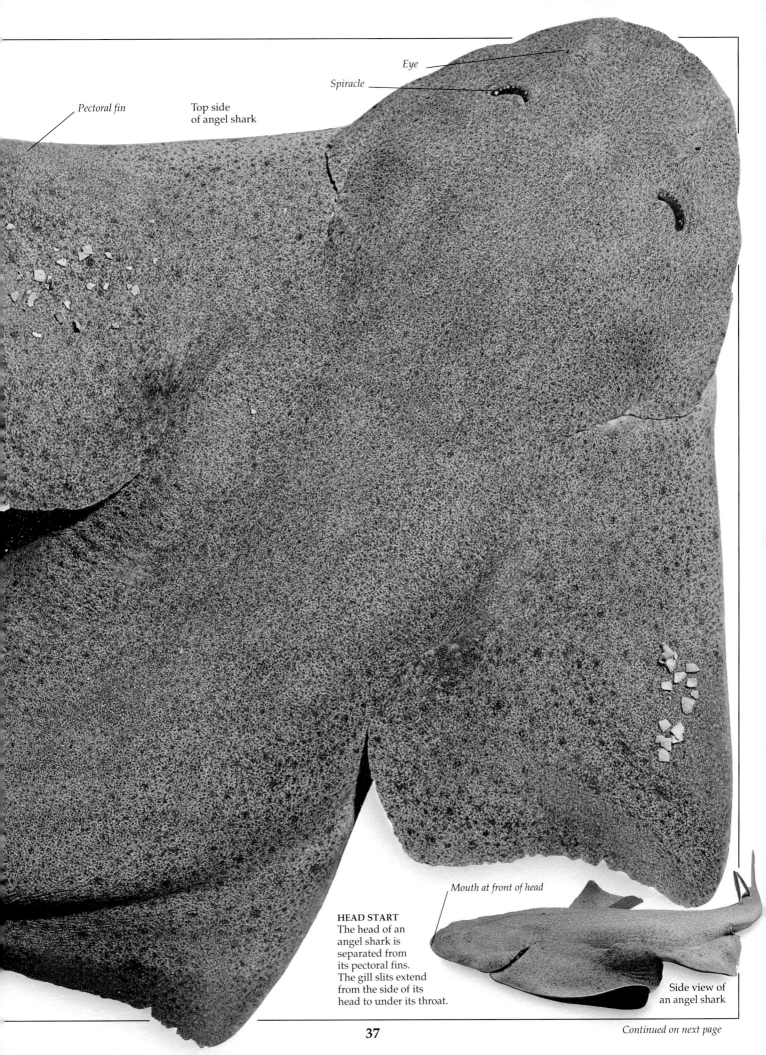

Eye

Spiracle

Pectoral fin

Top side
of angel shark

Continued on next page

Mouth at front of head

HEAD START
The head of an
angel shark is
separated from
its pectoral fins.
The gill slits extend
from the side of its
head to under its throat.

Side view of
an angel shark

37

SECRET AGENT
Spies work undercover on secret missions. Some kinds of shark are secretive too, and hide from predators by using camouflage.

ORIENTAL WOBBEGONG
This shark lives along the coasts of Japan, China, Vietnam, the Philippines, and Korea in the western Pacific. It grows to about 1 m (3.3 ft) in length. Wobbegongs are not normally aggressive, but people have been bitten when they have stepped on a wobbegong by mistake, because they are difficult to see. Fishermen have also been bitten by wobbegongs caught in their nets.

Japanese wobbegong

Lobe

Barbel

Undercover sharks

Sharks living on the sea bed like to hide. The colours and patterns on their skins help these sharks, such as wobbegong, swell, and angel sharks, to be camouflaged, or to blend in with their surroundings. They have blotches, spots, or stripes which make them difficult to see on sand, among rocks, seaweeds, or corals on the sea bed. Wobbegongs have elaborate disguises with blotchy skins and lobes on their heads which look like bits of seaweed. Other sharks, like swell sharks, hide in crevices, while angel sharks cover themselves with sand. Why hide if you are a shark with sharp teeth? These undercover sharks often lie in wait for prey, like fish and crabs, to move near, then snap them up. Also, hiding helps small sharks avoid being eaten by larger predators.

NOW YOU SEE ME, NOW YOU DON'T
It is difficult to see angel sharks (pp. 36–37) lying on the sea bed, because they are flattened and their mottled skin looks like sand (top left). To complete their superb disguise, angel sharks shuffle their pectoral fins to bury themselves in the sand (centre left). When hiding under a layer of sand, their eyes poke above the surface (bottom left) keeping watch for their prey like fish to swim by. When a fish comes near, the angel shark lunges forward, snapping its jaws shut around it. If divers approach, they may leave their hiding place and swim off. Fishermen catch angel sharks in nets towed across the sea bed.

AUSTRALIAN SHARK WITH A BEARD
The tasselled wobbegong's beard has many branched lobes around its mouth, which its prey, such as fish and shrimps, may mistake for seaweed and end up being eaten.

MUG SHOTS
Like a prisoner's mug shots, this ornate wobbegong looks different from different angles – from above (top left) and from the side (bottom left). The wobbegong's disguise works just as well from any direction. The Aborigines of Australia gave wobbegongs their wonderful name.

Predators may not see a swell shark because it is well camouflaged. But if attacked, it gulps down water, swelling up to jam itself into a crevice.

Ornate wobbegong

Barbel

WHERE'S THE TASSELLED WOBBEGONG?
Out of all six wobbegong species, this one has the most branched lobes, or tassels, on its head. Its beard extends around the mouth and down its chin.

A LIFE ON THE SEA BED
Wobbegongs spend much of the day lurking on the sea bed in the shallows and even in rockpools. They are flattened with their eyes and spiracles on the top of their head, just like angel sharks. All wobbegongs have an anal fin while angel sharks lack them. The lobes around their mouth are outgrowths of skin. Even the wobbegong's barbels, or whiskers, on its rounded snout look like fronds of seaweed.

Lobe

Horn sharks

Practising the horn makes perfect

HORN SHARKS GET THEIR NAME from the two spines on their backs next to each dorsal fin, which look like small horns. The sharks in this group are also called bullheads because they have broad heads with ridges above their eyes. The shape of the head and the presence of an anal fin distinguish horn sharks from spiny dogfish, which also have dorsal spines. There are eight species of horn shark. All are mostly less than 1.5 m (5 ft) long and are found in the Pacific and Indian Oceans, where they live on the sea bed in shallow water. Horn sharks swim with slow beats of their tails and push themselves along the bottom with their pectoral fins. The Australian Port Jackson sharks can travel long distances, covering 850 km (510 miles) to visit their breeding sites. Because horn sharks are slow, scuba divers sometimes tease them by pulling their tails – they have been known to bite back. Sadly, horn sharks are killed for their spines, used to make jewellery (pp. 60–61).

Pelvic fin

A pair of swimming Port Jackson sharks, which are named after an inlet in Australia

HEAP OF HORNS
Port Jackson sharks often share the same spot on the sea bed where they rest in groups during the day. Favourite rest sites are the sandy floors of caves or channels between rocks which may offer some protection against currents. As many as 16 sharks may share the same resting place. At night they become active searching for food such as sea urchins and starfish.

Spine in front of first dorsal fin

Caudal fin

Spine of second dorsal fin

Typical spotted pattern on skin

Eye

Side view of horn shark

Pelvic fin

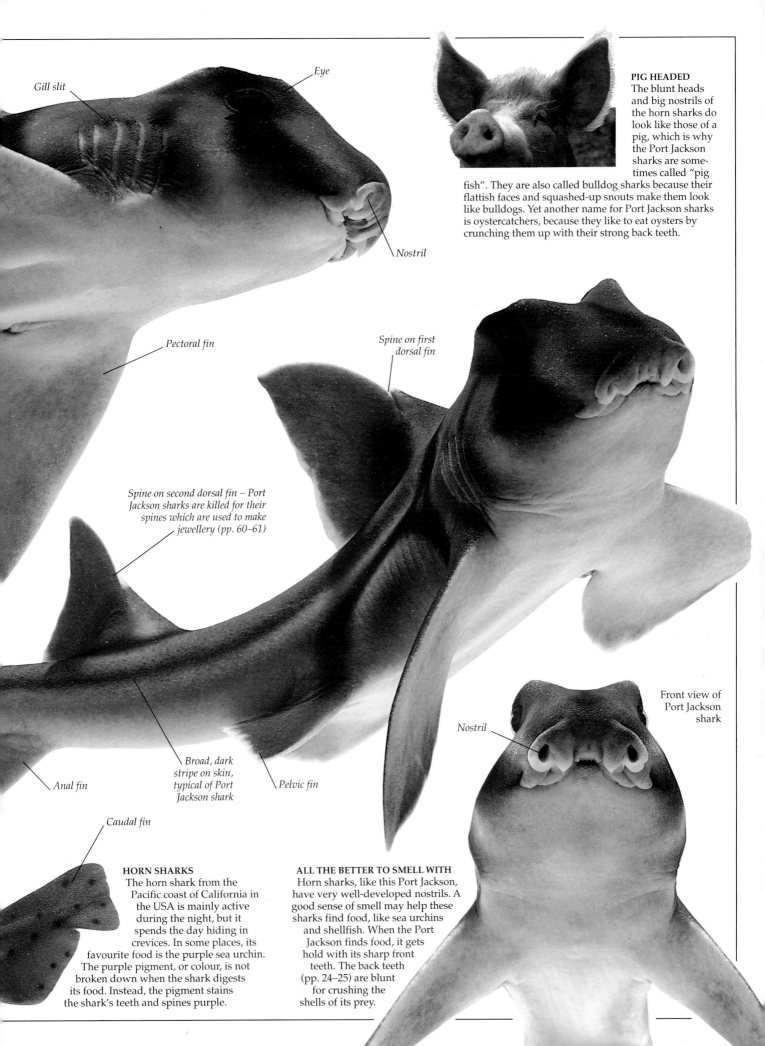

Gill slit

Eye

PIG HEADED
The blunt heads
and big nostrils of
the horn sharks do
look like those of a
pig, which is why
the Port Jackson
sharks are some-
times called "pig
fish". They are also called bulldog sharks because their
flattish faces and squashed-up snouts make them look
like bulldogs. Yet another name for Port Jackson sharks
is oystercatchers, because they like to eat oysters by
crunching them up with their strong back teeth.

Nostril

Pectoral fin

Spine on first
dorsal fin

Spine on second dorsal fin – Port
Jackson sharks are killed for their
spines which are used to make
jewellery (pp. 60–61)

Broad, dark
stripe on skin,
typical of Port
Jackson shark

Pelvic fin

Anal fin

Nostril

Front view of
Port Jackson
shark

Caudal fin

HORN SHARKS
The horn shark from the
Pacific coast of California in
the USA is mainly active
during the night, but it
spends the day hiding in
crevices. In some places, its
favourite food is the purple sea urchin.
The purple pigment, or colour, is not
broken down when the shark digests
its food. Instead, the pigment stains
the shark's teeth and spines purple.

ALL THE BETTER TO SMELL WITH
Horn sharks, like this Port Jackson,
have very well-developed nostrils. A
good sense of smell may help these
sharks find food, like sea urchins
and shellfish. When the Port
Jackson finds food, it gets
hold with its sharp front
teeth. The back teeth
(pp. 24–25) are blunt
for crushing the
shells of its prey.

Head like a hammer

OF ALL THE SHARKS, hammerheads have the strangest shaped heads. Included in the nine species of hammerhead are the bonnetheads, which only have small head projections. The winged hammerhead has by far the widest head, which can be half as long as its body. Most hammerhead species live in warm temperate and tropical coastal waters. The scalloped hammerhead is one of the most common species and occurs in warm waters throughout the world. Large schools of scalloped hammerheads congregate in some areas where there are features on the sea floor like undersea peaks, or sea mounts. A hundred of these sharks may form a school with them all swimming in unison. At dusk they swim off on their own to feed (pp. 18–19) and then at dawn they regroup in the same place.

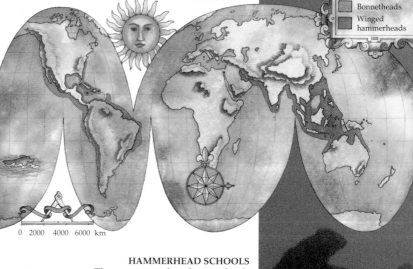

Distribution of hammerheads

Bonnetheads
Winged hammerheads

0 2000 4000 6000 km

HAMMERHEAD SCHOOLS
There are more females in schools than males, but the reason why they group together is unclear. These large predators have few enemies, so it is unlikely they school for protection. The females compete with each other (often butting one another) to stay in the centre of the schools. This may give them a better chance to be courted by the males.

DIFFICULT DIET
Stingrays are the favourite food of the great hammerhead even though they are armed with one or more venomous spines, or "stings", on their tails. Hammerheads do not seem to mind being stung – one individual had nearly a hundred spines sticking into its mouth and gullet.

TWO DIFFERENT SHARKS
The shape of the hammerhead's head (top) compared to that of other sharks – like the tope (bottom) – fascinated early naturalists.

A FINE BONNET
Bonnetheads are the smallest of the hammerheads, reaching only 1.5 m (5 ft) long compared to the great hammerhead, which can grow as much as 6 m (19.5 ft) long. They usually swim together in small groups, but sometimes huge schools of hundreds of sharks congregate near the surface.

First dorsal fin

Gill slit

Mouth

Pectoral fin

Bonnethead shark

Anal fin   *Pelvic fin*

WHY A HAMMER?
No-one knows why a hammerhead has a hammer-shaped head, but the broad, flattened head may give extra lift to the front of the shark's body as it swims. The two hammerheads (right) differ slightly in that the scalloped one (left) has an indentation in the middle of its head, while the smooth one does not.

HEAD ON

As hammerheads swim along, swinging their heads from side to side, they have an excellent all-round view as their eyes are at the tip of their hammers. Their broad heads bear many ampullae of Lorenzini, which sense tiny electric currents generated by their prey (pp. 18–19).

Scalloped hammerhead

Weird and wonderful

One of the world's most extraordinary sharks, the megamouth, was only discovered in 1976. No-one had come across this large shark before, although it is over 5 m (16 ft) long and weighs 680 kg (1500 lb). Since 1976 five more megamouths have been found, including one which was captured alive off the coast of California in 1990. Scientists attached radio tags to this living megamouth so they could follow it (pp. 54–55). The shark spent the day at 135–150 m (450–500 ft) down, feeding on "krill" (shrimp-like creatures). After sunset it rose up to within 12 m (40 ft) of the surface following its food source before its descent into the depths at dawn. Another strange shark, the goblin shark, was found nearly 100 years ago, yet scientists know little about it. Other mysteries have been solved. No-one knew what caused disc-shaped bites on whales, dolphins, and seals, but the culprits were found to be cookiecutter sharks. Who knows what other weird and wonderful sharks are still to be found deep in the ocean?

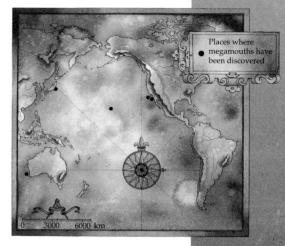

Places where megamouths have been discovered

0   3000   6000 km

BIG MOUTH
Megamouth means "big mouth", a good name for a shark with a 1-m (3-ft) grin. This shark may lure krill into its huge mouth with luminous organs around its lips. The first megamouth was brought up dead from 200 m (660 ft), entangled in the sea anchor of an American naval boat off Hawaii. The second was caught in gill nets (long nets in which fish are trapped) off California; the third was washed up and died on a beach near Perth, Australia; while a fourth was found dead and a fifth alive off the coast of Japan. The sixth was caught and released off the California coast.

Long snout with sensory pores for detecting prey

Goblin shark

Top side of goblin shark's head

Underside of goblin shark's head

REALLY WEIRD
These ugly sharks (above) were first discovered by scientists off the coast of Japan in 1898. They have flabby bodies and are over 3 m (10 ft) long. Not much is known about these rare sharks which live in deep water at least 160 m (530 ft) down.

Distribution of cookiecutters

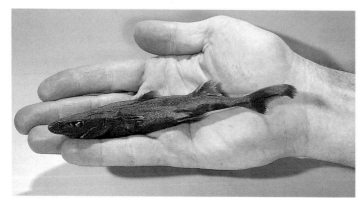

GLOWS IN THE DARK
This is one of the lantern sharks, which live in the oceans' dark depths. They are called lantern sharks because they are luminous, or glow in the dark. Among the world's smallest sharks, they grow to only 20 cm (8 in) long.

BITE SIZED

Cookiecutters have large teeth for sharks only 0.5 m (1.7 ft) long. The common cookiecutter (one of two species) uses its teeth to cut out chunks of flesh from large fish as well as whales, seals, and dolphins. It may wait for such large animals to come close rather than chasing after them. The cookiecutter forms a suction cup with its lips, then bites and swivels around to take an oval-shaped plug of flesh. Cookiecutters have also taken bites out of the rubber components of submarines and undersea cables.

GODDESS OF LIGHT

The cookiecutters' scientific name is after Isis, the Egyptian goddess of light. Cookiecutters have many light organs on their bellies and glow in the dark. This may attract prey like whales to come close enough to be bitten.

2000   4000   6000 km

BORING BITES

The wounds on this seal were made by a cookiecutter shark biting into its flesh.

Shark artefacts

MONKEY BUSINESS
This monkey-head was made by the Aztecs in Mexico. Made of precious stones, its teeth are those of a shark.

FOR CENTURIES, people around the world have caught sharks and taken their teeth and skin to make a wide variety of objects, or artefacts. Shark teeth are so sharp that early people were able to make tools and weapons from them. Shark skin is so hard-wearing that it could be used to make shoes, as well as grips or sheaths for swords and daggers (pp. 60–61). Early people who caught sharks had great respect for these magnificent predators. Fishing for sharks with primitive tools was difficult and dangerous, and stories and legends about sharks were common among seafaring and island people. Sharks were even regarded as gods and worshipped on some islands in the Pacific. In comparison, Europeans have few myths about sharks, but they did appear in natural history books (pp. 28–29).

Large, serrated tooth, probably from a great white shark (pp. 28–31)

CROWN JEWEL
The ten shark teeth that went into making this decorative necklace probably came from great white sharks caught off the coast of New Zealand, where the native Maoris live. Today's shark-tooth jewellery, made specially for tourists, contributes to the abuse, rather than the use, of sharks (pp. 60–61).

Pair of fisherman's shoes, made of shark skin, from India

Shark skin

Shark tooth

Shark-shaped gold weight from Ghana in West Africa

Tin toy, in the form of a shark, from Malaysia

Shark tooth

Tool, tipped with a shark's tooth, for tattooing people's skin, from Kiribati (the Gilbert Islands) in the western Pacific Ocean

Shark skin

Carved wooden drum, with shark-skin-covered top, 18th-century, from the Hawaiian Islands in the Pacific

Wooden rasp, covered in shark skin, from the island of Santa Cruz in the south-west Pacific

Shark skin

Shark-skin-covered grater (below) from the Wallis Islands in the Pacific

Wooden knife (right), with cutting edge made of sharks' teeth, from Greenland

Shark skin

SHARKS IN THE HOME
From ancient times, the skins and teeth of sharks have been used to make a variety of household items. Some shark skins are so rough that they have been used for grating food (left), but if the denticles are removed the soft skin is used like leather for making shoes and belts, or even drums (above). Shark teeth have been used for knives, jewellery, and tools. Other items were made in the shape of a shark because people admired sharks, but like today toy sharks were made just for fun.

FISHING AND WORSHIP

Early people often risked their lives, trying to catch sharks with primitive harpoons from small boats. Such heroic deeds often became a test of manhood. In some South Pacific islands, boys would go out in canoes to catch sharks for the island kings. They used rattles (right) to make noises in the water to attract sharks to their canoes. Then the sharks would be lured into a noose and killed with a club. The Hawaiian islanders fished for sharks and used both nooses and lines with hooks (below). They also believed that their dead relatives came back to life in the form of animals, such as sharks. These shark spirits would protect them while fishing. On other Pacific islands, sharks were thought of as gods and were never eaten.

Long spear for catching sharks, from the Nicobar Islands, India

Rattle made of coconut shells, for attracting sharks, near Samoa in the South Pacific

Small harpoon for catching sharks, The Gambia, West Africa

Sea spirit, with a shark-like head, from the Solomon Islands in the southwest Pacific

Shark-tooth necklace from New Zealand

Two hooks for catching sharks – one from Hawaii (right) is made of ivory, while the other (left) is carved in wood, from the Cook Islands in the southwest Pacific

Solomon Islanders believed a shark-shaped charm would keep large sharks out of their fishing nets (below)

Early 20th-century rattle, for attracting sharks, from Papua New Guinea, an island to the north of Australia

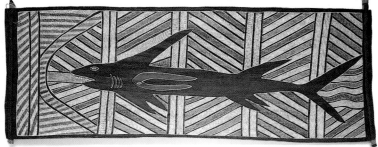

Turn upside down to find a dolphin

BARK PAINTING

The Australian Aborigines painted designs on pieces of bark cut from trees. In their painting, they often reveal what is inside an animal. In this 20th-century bark painting (left), the painter shows the shark's liver, which has two large lobes.

Shark tooth

SHARK WEAPONS

Sharp shark teeth were used by people from the Pacific islands as weapons for cutting and slashing their opponents. They made knuckle dusters and gloves (right) as well as swords, using rows of shark teeth as a cutting edge, instead of metal. Shark skin was used in other parts of the world, such as Africa and the Middle East, to make scabbards for protecting metal swords (below).

Shark tooth

Early Hawaiians packed a punch with this shark-tooth knuckle duster

A warrior from Kiribati would put his fingers into the loops of this glove, to cover his forearm with rows of teeth

Sword used by the Ashanti tribe from Ghana in West Africa

Shark-skin-covered sheath, or scabbard

Gold-plated handle

Shark attack

Mᴏsᴛ sʜᴀʀᴋs are not dangerous and leave people alone. Sharks attack about 50 to 75 people each year in the world, but only 5 to 10 of these reported attacks result in death. People are more likely to die in car accidents or drown in the sea than be killed by a shark. Attacks may occur when a shark mistakes a person for its normal prey, biting a foot that looks like a fish. A shark may attack if it feels threatened or is provoked. It is dangerous to be in water where there may be sharks: if the water is murky, if you have cut yourself, or if bait has been put out for fish. Always take advice if there are sharks in the area – never swim alone or at night.

ATTACK AT SEA
Prisoners, escaping from Devil's Island off Guyana, are attacked by sharks.

GREAT WHITE SHARK
Ever since the *Jaws* movies, the great white has had a reputation as a blood-thirsty killer. They do attack and kill people but this may be because they mistake them for their natural prey. Surfers are at risk near breeding grounds of elephant seals and sea lions, where great whites like to hunt.

WOUNDED SEAL
Elephant seals are what most great whites on the California coast like to sink their teeth into. These sharks usually approach their prey from behind to take a bite out of it. Then they wait until the victim is weakened from loss of blood before finishing it off. Sometimes the seal escapes by managing to reach the beach before the shark attacks again.

FATAL SHARK ATTACK
Most fatal shark attacks occur where people surf, swim, or scuba dive, and where there are large sharks, like the great white, swimming close to shore. Attacks can also occur on people escaping from sinking ships or plane crashes far out to sea. Each year the International Shark Attack File records the numbers of attacks reported.

Each year an average of 92 people die by drowning in the sea off Australia's coast . . .

. . . while around eight people die from scuba diving accidents . . .

. . . and less than one person dies from a shark attack.

WARNING SIGN
To avoid being attacked by sharks, take note of signs like this Australian one. Sharks attack people wading in shallow water.

BULL SHARK
Bull sharks are one of the four most dangerous sharks in the world, along with the great white, oceanic white tip, and tiger sharks. The bull shark lives in the warm waters of the world's oceans. It is one of the few sharks that spends time in fresh water, swimming far up rivers such as South America's Amazon and Africa's Zambezi. They can also enter lakes. At 3 m (10 ft) long, they are large enough to tackle a person and are not fussy what they eat.

NORTH AMERICA

Boston
New York

San Francisco
San Diego

PACIFIC OCEAN

FLORIDA

HAWAIIAN ISLANDS

SOUTH AMERICA

0   2000   4000   6000 km

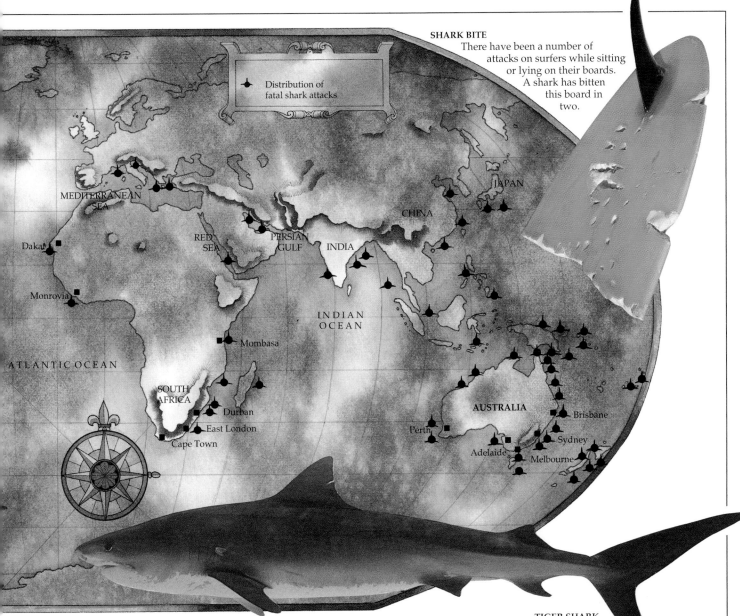

SHARK BITE
There have been a number of attacks on surfers while sitting or lying on their boards. A shark has bitten this board in two.

Distribution of fatal shark attacks

MEDITERRANEAN SEA

JAPAN

CHINA

Dakar

RED SEA

PERSIAN GULF

INDIA

Monrovia

INDIAN OCEAN

ATLANTIC OCEAN

Mombasa

SOUTH AFRICA

AUSTRALIA

Durban

Brisbane

East London

Perth

Sydney

Cape Town

Adelaide

Melbourne

DUMMY ATTACK
Wet suits do not protect against shark attack as this experiment with a dummy shows, nor do coloured or patterned wet suits repel sharks.

SHARK'S EYE VIEW
Attacks on surfers occur near seal or sea lion breeding colonies, when surfers have dangled their arms or legs over the edge of their surf boards. Sharks can mistake surfers for seals because they have similar shapes when seen from below.

TIGER SHARK
Tiger sharks eat almost anything, from turtles, seals, jellyfish, dolphins, sea birds, sea snakes, and junk like tin cans. They may be tempted to eat any animal, including people, that might make another meal.

NORMAL SWIMMING
Grey reef sharks live near coral reefs in the Indian and Pacific Oceans and grow to about 2.5 m (8 ft) long. When swimming normally, the back is gently curved and the pectoral fins held straight out from the body.

THREAT POSTURE
If a diver approaches too close or surprises a grey reef shark, it may adopt this threat posture. The shark arches its back and holds its pectoral fins downwards. It may also swim around in a figure of eight. If the diver does not swim slowly away, the shark may attack.

Sharks at bay

JONAH AND THE ?
In the bible story, Jonah was swallowed by a large sea creature, which could have been a shark, rather than a whale.

PEOPLE WHO GO into the water where there may be dangerous sharks run a small risk of being attacked. There is no simple way to keep sharks away from all the places where people paddle, swim, surf, or scuba dive. Shark-proof enclosures have been built but these can only protect small areas because of the large cost. In South Africa and Australia, nets are used along the most popular beaches to trap sharks. These nets also trap and kill many harmless sharks, dolphins, rays, and turtles. Tests are being done to see if electric barriers can be used which would keep sharks away without killing them or other animals. Scuba divers may, occasionally, carry bangsticks (tipped with an explosive cartridge), but often an inquisitive shark can be simply pushed away with a long, sturdy stick or club. If all else fails, kicking or punching a shark's snout may put them off an attack.

LIFE GUARDS
Australian life guards look out for sharks. If sharks are spotted near a beach, the shark alarm is sounded and swimmers leave the water. The beach may be closed for the rest of the day, if sharks stay in the area. Always follow a life guard's advice on safe swimming.

BLOWN AWAY!
A tiger shark is brought aboard after being killed with a bangstick. The stick fires on contact, tearing apart the shark's insides.

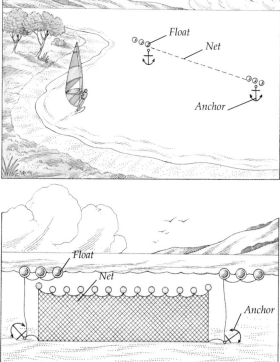

Float
Net
Anchor

Float
Net
Anchor

IN THE BAG
One way to help people who end up in the sea if a ship sinks or an aeroplane crashes, is to give them large, inflatable bags. When tested by the US Navy, sharks avoided them, because they could not see any limbs, sense any electric signals, or smell blood or body wastes, which are kept in the bag.

ONE LESS SHARK
A shark, trapped in a mesh net off an Australian beach (right), is landed. In the 1930s during a 17-month period, 1500 sharks were caught by this method. Since then numbers of sharks have decreased sharply.

NETTING BEACHES
Mesh nets are used to protect the most popular beaches by trapping sharks in the area. The nets do not form a continuous barrier, so sharks may be caught on both sides of the nets – either swimming towards or away from the beach. Heavy anchors keep the nets on or close to the bottom and floats keep the top of the net suspended in the water. The nets are about 100 m (330 ft) long and 6 m (20 ft) deep. Marker buoys float at the surface so the nets are easily found again. The nets are checked almost every day and dead sea animals removed. After three weeks the nets need to be replaced because they become fouled by seaweed and other marine growth, and so can easily be seen and avoided by sharks. Nets that have become tangled up in storm waves also need to be replaced.

CHAIN WALL

This wall (left) of interlinked chains surrounding an Australian beach prevents any sharks from getting in. Such walls are too costly to protect more than a few kilometres of beach. Chemical repellants have also been tried but they are not effective, as any substance released around a person in the water disperses too quickly in the waves.

PROTECTED BEACH

Experiments using screens made of bubbles released from air hoses on the sea bed have been carried out, but shark nets, as on this Australian beach (above), still seem to offer the best protection.

INVISIBLE BARRIER

Sharks are very sensitive to electric currents and here an invisible electric barrier is being tested. When the current is off (top) the lemon shark swims past, but when the current is switched on (left) the shark turns back to avoid it. Cables and even portable devices that produce electrical pulses to deter sharks have been tested in the sea.

DEATH NETS

Mesh nets, used to protect beaches, kill many sharks each year, like the great white (above) and hammerhead (left). Sharks entangled in nets are not able to swim and suffocate because they cannot keep water flowing over their gills. Up to 1400 sharks, many of them harmless, as well as dolphins, are caught each year in South African nets.

SHARK REPELLANT

The American scientist, Dr. Eugenie Clark, discovered that the moses sole from the Red Sea produces its own shark repellant. When attacked, milky secretions ooze out of pores on its skin, causing the shark to spit it out.

Studying sharks

HMS CHALLENGER
This British research vessel took 19th-century naturalists to the Atlantic, Pacific, and Indian Oceans, where all kinds of marine life including sharks were collected.

IN THE WILD, it is difficult to study sharks because they constantly move around, swim too fast and dive too deep for divers to keep up with them. Some sharks, like hammerheads, are even scared away by bubbles produced by scuba divers. To follow sharks, scientists catch them and attach sonic tags to their fins. When the sharks are released, scientists can keep track of them by picking up radio signals with a receiver.

Great care is taken to keep sharks alive, when they are caught for tagging and other studies. Also, certain types of shark are captured and placed in aquariums where they can be easily observed (pp. 62–63).

Sonic tag

Tagging pole loaded with dart tag

Dart ready for insertion

Return address label

Dr. McCosker tracking sharks in Australia

Propeller measuring a shark's swimming speed is attached to fin of a mako shark

STUDYING LEMONS
Dr. Samuel Gruber has studied lemon sharks in the Bahamas for over 10 years. They do not mind being handled and do not need to swim to breathe, so they can be kept still while scientists make their observations. In this experiment (right), a substance is being injected into the shark to show how fast it can grow. Young lemons too can have tiny tags inserted in their dorsal fins and are identified later by their own personal code number.

GETTING UP A SHARK'S NOSE
American scientist Dr. Samuel Gruber checks the flow of water through this nurse shark's nose. Scientists have to be careful because, although nurse sharks are normally docile, they can give a nasty bite (pp. 18–19).

SCIENTISTS' FAVOURITE
Lemon sharks are one of the easiest sharks to study, both in aquariums and in the sea. A young lemon shark (left) attacks her food. When she eats, she shakes her head vigorously, creating a large amount of debris in the aquarium's water.

TAGGING TIGERS
Scientists tag a small tiger shark in the Bahamas (top). Sometimes sharks need to be revived after this, so a diver (above) is pushing a large tiger shark along to keep water flowing over its gills.

KEEPING DRY
To go underwater without getting wet, American naturalist Prof. W. Beebe (1877–1962) used this bathysphere in the 1930s to reach a depth of 1000 m (3300 ft). Sharks, as deep as 3600 m (12,000 ft), are attracted by bait.

THE FRILL OF IT ALL
Three of these strange sharks (below) were caught off Japan in deep water during the 1870s' *Challenger* expedition.

Frilled shark

Sixth gill slit – most sharks have only five

Tagging sharks

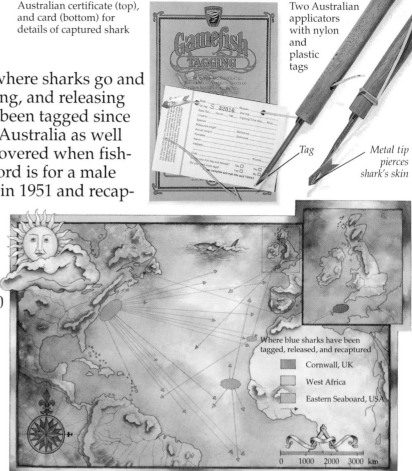

Australian certificate (top), and card (bottom) for details of captured shark

Two Australian applicators with nylon and plastic tags

Tag

Metal tip pierces shark's skin

ANGLERS CAN HELP SCIENTISTS find out where sharks go and how fast they grow by measuring, tagging, and releasing them. Tens of thousands of sharks have been tagged since the 1950s, off the coasts of the USA and Australia as well as the UK and Africa. A few tags are recovered when fishermen catch these sharks again. The record is for a male Australian tope, which was first tagged in 1951 and recaptured in 1986, 214 km (130 miles) from its original release site. Its length had increased by 17 cm (7 in). Blue sharks are among the greatest ocean travellers. One tagged near New York was caught 16 months later off Brazil, 6000 km (3600 miles) away, while another tagged off the UK's Devon coast was recaptured off Brazil, 7000 km (4200 miles) away.

Where blue sharks have been tagged, released, and recaptured

■ Cornwall, UK

□ West Africa

→ Eastern Seaboard, USA

0   1000   2000   3000 km

BIRD RINGING
Ringing bands around young birds' legs gives information on migration – just as tags do for sharks – if they are caught again.

Bait

1 TAGGING/RELEASING SHARKS
Like most sharks, blue sharks have an excellent sense of smell and are attracted to boats by dangling a chum bag containing smelly, salted fish over the side. The chum's oil spreads out in a thin film over the water's surface, attracting sharks from a great distance. The shark hooks are baited with freshly caught mackerel and the fishing lines are let out to depths of 12–18 m (40–60 ft).

2 HOOKED
Attracted by the oil and blood, the blue shark has taken the bait.

3 REELING IN
The shark is reeled in near the boat, very carefully, so as not to damage the shark.

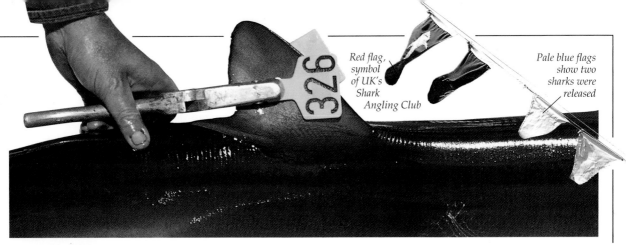

6 TAGGING DORSAL FIN
The tag is made of strong metal which will not corrode in sea water and cause the plastic numbered tag to drop out. On the reverse side of the tag is an address to where the tag can be sent, should another angler or fisherman catch the tagged shark again in another part of the world.

Red flag, symbol of UK's Shark Angling Club

Pale blue flags show two sharks were released

7 RELEASING
Holding the shark by her tail, the skipper gently lowers her back into the sea. Once in the water, the shark swims away as fast as she can.

5 HOLDING THE SHARK DOWN
This female blue shark is 1.5 m (5 ft) long and weighs about 22.5 kg (50 lb). The skipper holds her down and gets ready to insert the tag. The shark can tolerate being out of the water for only a few minutes, so he has to work quickly to put the tag into her dorsal fin. Buckets of salt water are thrown onto the shark to help keep her alive. In other tagging studies, the shark is brought close to the boat and not landed to help avoid damaging it. Then a pole is used to stick the tag into the shark (pp. 28–29).

4 THRESHING SHARK
The skipper begins to haul the threshing shark in, but it fights every bit of the way.

Shark overkill

PEOPLE KILL SHARKS for their meat, fins, skin, and liver oil, as well as for pure sport. Sport fishing can reduce numbers of sharks locally, but the biggest threat to sharks is overfishing worldwide. Sharks, caught on long lines and in fishing nets, are often thrown back into the sea dead, because it is other fish hauled in at the same time that are wanted. Sometimes just the shark's fins are removed and its body thrown back. Sharks are also killed each year in nets to protect swimmers. Compared to bony fish, sharks have a much slower rate of reproduction and take a long time to mature. If too many are killed, their numbers may never recover. Efforts are now being made to protect sharks by creating reserves, restricting numbers caught, and banning fishing.

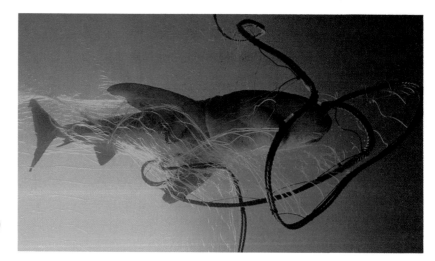

ANGLING
Angling is a popular sport. Fast, strong sharks represent a big challenge. Today, angling clubs are becoming more aware of conservation and some are restricting the size of shark that can be landed. Increasingly, anglers are encouraged to release sharks, instead of killing them (pp. 56–57).

WALLS OF DEATH
Drift nets (top), some 15 m (50 ft) deep and many kilometres long, are used to catch fish. The nets are so fine that fish do not see them and become trapped in the mesh. Sharks, like this oceanic white-tipped shark (above), are easily caught, along with seabirds, turtles, and dolphins.

WHITE DEATH
For many anglers, the great white (above) is the ultimate trophy. People are frightened of great whites and so kill them, but among the sea's top predators, these sharks are important in keeping the natural balance in the ocean. The hunting of great whites is banned in South Africa. In Australia, they may become a protected species.

SPORT OR SLAUGHTER
To show just how many sharks were killed, this hunter's boat (left) shows a collection of the victims' jaws.

Drift net

THRASHED THRESHER
Thresher sharks (left) are heavily fished in both the Pacific and Indian Oceans. They are caught with long lines and gill nets. Landing a thresher can be dangerous, especially if they lash out with their tails. Sometimes their tails get hooked on long lines.

SAD END FOR A TIGER
The tiger shark (right) was killed in an angling competition in Florida, USA. Near some coastal resorts, the numbers of large, predatory sharks – like the great white and tiger – have declined, probably due to the large numbers being caught by anglers.

FISHING FOR FOOD
In developing countries, people, like these Asians (left), depend on shark meat for protein. In other countries, shark is often a luxury food in restaurants. Whether we choose to eat shark or not, it is important that shark fishing is controlled. If not, these fascinating creatures could disappear from the world's oceans.

Cutting up sharks for meat

DRYING FINS
Shark fins are used in Chinese cooking for delicacies like shark fin soup. Because the fins can be dried, they are much easier to market than shark meat, which has to be sold quickly or processed.

Shark fins drying

FINNING
These Japanese fishermen on a boat in the Pacific Ocean are cutting the fins off sharks caught in drift nets. They throw the rest of the shark back in the sea. Fins of many different kinds of shark are removed, sometimes when they are still alive. When thrown back in the sea, they take a long time to die. Without their fins, they are not able to swim properly and may be torn apart by other sharks.

Use and abuse

PEOPLE HAVE FOUND A USE for almost every part of a shark's body. The tough skin can be turned into leather, the teeth into jewellery, the jaws into souvenirs, the carcass into fertilizers, the fins into soup, the flesh eaten, and the oil from the liver used in industry, medicines, and cosmetics. Human exploitation of wild animals like sharks can cause a serious decline in numbers, if more animals are killed than can be replaced by the birth and survival of the young. Sharks are especially at risk because they are slow to reproduce. It is hard to put sensible limits on the numbers of shark that can safely be fished because so little is known about them. Today, sharks are mainly exploited for their meat and fins and demand for shark meat will probably continue as the human population increases. If fewer people were to use products derived from sharks, their future would be more secure. Otherwise, the effect on the natural balance in the oceans could prove to be disastrous.

SHARK TEETH
These pendants are made from the teeth of the great white shark. Misguided people think that wearing shark tooth pendants make them look as fierce as a great white.

NAPOLEON AND THE SHARK
Sailors feared and disliked sharks. Here, the French emperor Napoleon (1769–1821) watches a shark being killed, during his journey into exile on the remote Atlantic island of St. Helena.

GETTING A GRIP
This sword handle, covered with rough shark skin, gives a swordsman a secure grip.

In battle, a bloody handle could still be gripped

The shark skin on the handle of this British Royal Artillery officer's sword has been dyed

Rough ray skin under black cord

SAMURAI SWORD
This 19th-century sword once belonged to a Samurai warrior from Japan. Its handle is covered with unpolished ray skin, while the sheath is made of the polished and lacquered skin of a ray (pp. 8–9).

Carved ivory handle

Lacquered ray-skin-covered sheath

PERSIAN DAGGER
The sheath of this 19th-century Persian dagger is covered in ray skin. A flowery design has been painted onto the lacquered skin.

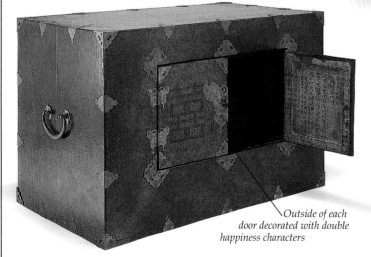

BOX OF HAPPINESS
Fine shark skin, or leather, was used to cover this early 20th-century rectangular box from Korea. The leather is smooth because the denticles, or small teeth, have been highly polished, then lacquered, and dyed dark green. Shagreen – rough, unpolished shark skin – is used as an abrasive, like sandpaper, for polishing wood.

Outside of each door decorated with double happiness characters

SHARK REMAINS
These two hammer-heads (pp. 42–43) were caught off the coast of the Baja Peninsula in western Mexico. In this poor area, their meat was probably used for food and their skin for making into leather goods, such as wallets and belts.

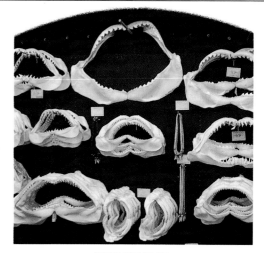

JAWS FOR SALE
Many sharks are killed and their jaws sold to tourists as souvenirs. Jaws of large sharks, like the great white (pp. 28–31), fetch high prices. The sale of great white jaws is now banned in South Africa.

SHARK AND CHIPS
Much of the fish sold in British fish and chip shops is, in fact, spiny dogfish (pp. 22–23), one of the most abundant and heavily fished kinds of shark. Many kinds of shark are given a different name when sold for meat – dogfish is disguised as "rock salmon" in Britain. In the past, people did not like to eat shark because they thought sharks ate the bodies of dead sailors. Sadly, shark steaks are becoming a fashionable delicacy in some restaurants.

HEADLESS CORPSE
This shark was killed for sport and had its head cut off so its jaws could be removed. Shark jaws are popular trophies in the same way that hunters show off the head and horns of deer they have shot.

SHARK LIVER OIL PILLS
In some countries people believe that shark oil can cure all kinds of ills. Shark oil is composed of many different substances, including vitamin A, but this vitamin can now be made artificially.

Polished, lacquered ray skin

A cluster of shark liver oil pills

Two bowls and a tin of an oriental delicacy – shark fin soup

SHARK FIN SOUP
The cartilaginous fibres in shark fins are made into soup, which some oriental people regard as a delicacy. The dried fins are soaked and repeatedly boiled to extract the mass of gelatinous fibres. Many other ingredients are then added to these noodle-like fibres to give the soup some taste.

SKIN CARE
Shark oil is used in costly skin creams that are meant to prevent wrinkles and signs of aging. But other creams based on natural plant oils are just as effective.

Save the shark!

SHARKS HAVE A BAD reputation as blood-thirsty killers. But only a few kinds of shark are dangerous (pp. 48–49) and attacks on people are rare. Other animals like tigers, and even elephants, which also occasionally kill people, are more popular. People need to be concerned about sharks because they are increasingly threatened by overfishing (pp. 58–59). Some sharks, like lemon sharks in Florida, in the USA, also suffer because of the destruction of mangrove swamps which are important nurseries for their pups. To begin to like sharks, people need to learn all about them. By visiting an aquarium, everyone can see the grace and beauty of sharks. Good swimmers can learn to snorkel and scuba dive, and may be lucky enough to see sharks in the sea. In some areas, like California in the USA, scuba divers are taken on trips to specific places where they can observe truly wild sharks.

MAD ON SHARKS
This crazy sculpture of a blue shark on the roof of a house near Oxford, England, shows just how much some people like sharks.

Making sketches of various sharks in an aquarium

TANKS FOR THE VIEW
Seeing sharks come within centimetres of your nose is a great thrill, even if there is a glass wall in between (right). But not all kinds of shark can be kept in aquariums. The fast-moving blue sharks and makos are used to roaming over great distances and need much more space than there is in an aquarium. A great white shark was once kept in an aquarium for a few days, but it became disorientated, continually hitting its nose against the glass, so it had to be released back into the sea. Smaller sharks, like smooth-hounds (pp. 14–15), are the easiest to keep in an aquarium.

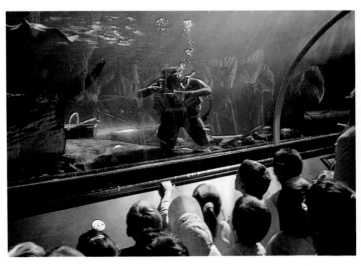

Face to face with a shark (right) and feeding time at the aquarium (far right)

*Sand
tiger
shark*

*White
tip reef
shark*

*Bull
huss*

Photographs
taken in an
aquarium

CANDID CAMERA
Taking photographs
of sharks in aquariums
is a good way to start
getting to know them.
Photographing moving
subjects behind glass is not
easy, but perseverance will pay
off. Use a film with a fast speed,
because aquariums have little
light. Ask permission to photograph,
but do not use a flash if there are signs
prohibiting this. Hold the camera flat against
the side of a tank to prevent light bouncing off
the glass, if using a flash. Wait for the whole body
of the shark to come into view before taking a
photograph, but remember that it moves fast!

LEARNING ABOUT SHARKS
Join a conservation organization that works to help protect
marine life in the oceans and seas. Look out for infor-
mative articles in wildlife magazines and for other
books about sharks. There are also interesting under-
water programmes on television which, unlike the
scary *Jaws* movies, tell the real story about sharks.
Aim to volunteer to help marine biologists in their
research programmes, like the Earthwatch research
in the Bahamas in the Caribbean. There is still so
much more to be discovered about sharks.

*A sketch of a classic requiem shark,
with its streamlined body and highly
efficient system of movement that
complements its predatory lifestyle*

*A typical mackerel
shark, which is
stouter than a
requiem shark*

Sketching sharks
can be fun as
well as useful

SHARKS ON FILE
Visiting aquariums, keeping a shark notebook,
drawing pictures of sharks, or copying them from
photographs, are good ways of seeing how many
different kinds of sharks there are. Compare the
sharks' colours, variety of skin patterns, and the
different body shapes. Eventually, a valuable shark
information file can be built up. Note down the
size, diet, natural habitat, and how the various
sharks differ. On sketches, label their external
features, like fins, gill slits, eyes, and
mouth. With some effort, anyone
can become more of an expert
on sharks.

*Noting down your
observations can help
build up a valuable
shark information file*

Pastels

Pencils

Index

Acknowledgements

Dorling Kindersley would like to thank:
Alan Hills, John Williams, and Mike Row of the British Museum, Harry Taylor and Tim Parmenter of the Natural History Museum, Michael Dent, and Michael Pitts (Hong Kong) for additional special photography. The staff of Sea Life Centres (UK), especially Robin James and Ed Speight (Weymouth) and Rod Haynes (Blackpool), David Bird (Poole Aquarium), and Ocean Park Aquarium (Hong Kong), for providing specimens for photography and species information.
The staff of the British Museum, Museum of Mankind, the Natural History Museum, especially Oliver Crimmen of the Fish Dept, the Marine Biological Association (UK), the Marine Conservation Society (UK), Sarah Fowler of the Nature Conservation Bureau (UK), the Sydney Aquarium (Darling Harbour, Australia), John West of the Aust. Shark Attack File (Taronga Zoo, Australia), George Burgess of the International Shark Attack File (Florida Museum of Natural History, USA), Dr. Peter Klimley (University of California, USA), and Rolf Williams for their research help.

Djutja Djutja Munuygurr, Djapu artist, 1983/1984, for bark painting. John Reynolds and the *Ganesha* (Cornwall) for the tagging sequence. Oliver Denton and Carly Nicolls as photographic models.
Peter Bailey, Katie Davis (Australia), Muffy Dodson (Hong Kong), Chris Howson, Earl Neish, Manisha Patel, and Helena Spiteri for their design and editorial assistance.
Jane Parker for the index.

Maps Sallie Alane Reason
Illustrations John Woodcock

Picture credits
t=top, b=bottom, c=centre, l=left, r=right
Ardea: Jack Daniels 41 tr; Mark Heiches 52bl; D Parer & E Parer-Cook 19tc; Peter Steyn 8b, 30bc; Ron & Valerie Taylor 7br, 18cl, 19tl, 25bc, 38bl, 40cl, 49ct, 52t, 52bc, 53tr, 53t, 53cr, 53br; Valerie Taylor 19bl, 31, 51c, 51bl, 60tr; Wardene Weisser 8c.
Aviation Picture Library/Austin J Brown: 35br.
The British Museum/Museum of Mankind: 46tl.
Bridgeman: The Prado (Madrid), *The Tooth Extractor* by Theodor Rombouts (1597-1637), 32bl; Private Collection, *The Little Mermaid* by E S Hardy, 21tl.
Capricorn Press Pty: 51t, 56tl, 56tr.
J Allan Cash: 27br, 50tr, 51tlb.
Bruce Coleman Ltd: 59c.
Neville Coleman's Underwater Geographic

Photo Agency: 20cr, 61cr.
Ben Cropp (Australia): 50ct, 50b.
C M Dixon: 47cr.
Dorling Kindersley: Colin Keates 25tr, 32br; Kim Taylor 21tl; Jerry Young, 9cr, 42cr.
Richard Ellis (USA): 17r.
Perry Gilbert (USA): 51tr, 51trb.
Peter Goadby (Australia): 28t.
Greenpeace: 58tr; 59br.
T Britt Griswold: 44b.
Tom Haight (USA): 45t.
Sonia Halliday & Laura Lushington: 50tl.
Robert Harding Picture Library: 18tr.
Edward S Hodgson (USA): 61bl.
Eric & David Hosking: 56cl.
The Hulton Picture Company: front cover ct, 34tl, 42cl.
Hunterian Museum (Glasgow): 13c.
The Image Bank/Guido Alberto Rossi: 30t.
Intervideo Television Clip Entertainment Group Ltd: 6t.
F Jack Jackson: 49cr, 49br.
C Scott Johnson (USA): 50cb.
Stéphane Korb (France): 58cr, 58b.
Frank Lane Picture Agency: 30br.
Eric Le Feuvre (USA): 20br.
William MacQuitty: 45bc.
Mary Evans Picture Library: front cover br, 10t, 36t, 38t, 40t, 48tl, 52tl, 55br, 60tl.
National Museum of Natural History, Smithsonian Institution (Washington, DC): Photo Chip Clark 13r.
NHPA: Joe B Blossom 23cr; John Shaw 23tl; ANT/Kelvin Aitken 48cr.
National Marine Fisheries Service: H Wes Pratt 54ct, 59tl; Greg Skomal 54bl; Charles Stillwell 23tc, 23tr.

Ocean Images: Rosemary Chastney 28b, 29b, 29c, 54cl; Walt Clayton 15br, 49cl; Al Giddings 15cr, 45br, 48cl, 49bl, 53bl; Charles Nicklin 29br; Doc White 20cl, 20bcl.
Oxford Scientific Films: Fred Bavendam 25cl, 39b; Tony Crabtree 34b, 35t; Jack Dermid 25cr; Max Gibbs 27cbr; Rudie Kuiter 43bl; Godfrey Merlen 43br; Peter Parks 35c; Kim Westerskov inside front cover tr, 49tr; Norbert Wu 45cr.
Planet Earth Pictures: Richard Cook 59bl; Walter Deas 24bc, 39c, 48bl; Daniel W Gotsholl 30cl; Jack Jackson 51br; Robert A Jureit 22c, 22cr, 23c, 23cl; A Kerstitch 21cr, 21bc, 21b; Ken Lucas 20tr, 24cr, 39tr, 42bl; Krov Menhuin 27bl; D Murrel 32t; Doug Perrine front cover cbl, 22cl, 23br, 25t, 26bc, 54br, 55tr, 55cr; Christian Petron 42br; Brian Pitkin 24tl; Flip Schulke 30tl; Marty Snyderman 20bl, 27t, 42t, 43t, 54cr; James P Watt 32t, 32b, 33t, 33b; Marc Webber 30bl; Norbert Wu 26c, 48br.
Courtesy of Sea Life Centres (UK): 62bl.
Shark Angling Club of Great Britain: 58cl.
Courtesy of Sydney Aquarium (Darling Harbour, Australia): 62br.
Werner Forman Archive/Museum of Mankind: 47cl.
Courtesy of Wilkinson Sword: 60cl.
Rolf Williams: 16tl, 18cr (in block of six), 59tr, 61tr.

Every effort has been made to trace the copyright holders. Dorling Kindersley apologizes for any unintentional omissions and would be pleased, in such cases, to add an acknowledgement in future editions.